EXPLORERS

in

Early Texas

EXPLORERS
in
Early Texas

Written and Illustrated
by
Betsy Warren

Hendrick-Long Publishing Company
Dallas

THANK YOU
to all the librarians at Howson Branch and Barker History Center in Austin who helped me find information for this book.

Library of Congress Cataloging-in-Publication Data

Warren, Betsy
   Explorers in early Texas / written and illustrated by Betsy Warren.
       p.   cm.
   Includes bibliographical references and index.
   Summary: Discusses the Spanish and French explorations of what is now Texas, between 1519 and 1778, by Alonso Piñeda, Cabeza de Vaca, Coronado, La Salle, Terán, and Mézières.
   ISBN 0-937460-74-5
   1. Texas—Discovery and exploration—Juvenile literature. 2. Explorers—Texas—History—Juvenile literature. 3. Texas—History—To 1846—Juvenile literature. [1. Texas—Discovery and exploration. 2. Texas—History—To 1846. 3. Explorers.] I. Title.
F389.W34 1992   91-4187
976.4'01—dc20   CIP
                                                          AC

ISBN 0-937460-74-5 (hc)
ISBN 1-885777-12-4 (sc)
5432
Copyright © 1992 Hendrick-Long Publishing Company
P.O. Box 12311
Dallas, TX 75225

Contents

A Note from the Author

The land of Texas had no name when the first Spanish explorers came to its shores. Neither did it have any definite boundary lines. After returning home, the travelers described the area to the king of Spain. He declared that it would be called "Amichel." During the next three hundred years as more explorers arrived and trekked over the land, the name was changed many times.

The one name that endured was an Indian word which means "Friends" or "Allies." Since the Indians had no alphabet or spelling, the Spaniards had to write the sound as well as they could. After being spelled several different ways, such as Tayshas, Téjas, Techas, Tecas, it finally became Texas.

In order to lessen confusion for readers, the maps and stories of this book will use the present-day contours of the state and the name *Texas* to designate the expanse of land crossed by the early explorers.

ALONSO PIÑEDA
1494(?)-1519

Four ships set sail to the west from the island of
Jamaica in the year 1519. From their tall masts, the
flag of Spain fluttered in the light spring breeze. On
board the ships were 270 adventurous men—sailors,
soldiers, civil servants, and a few priests. The captain,
ALONSO PIÑEDA, was proceeding under orders
from Governor Garay of Jamaica.

compass

"No one has ever charted a good map of the Gulf of
Mexico," the governor had said to Piñeda. "It's time
that one is made. I have chosen you to chart the coastline of the gulf from Florida to Veracrúz in Mexico.
Also, be on the lookout for a waterway that might be a
passage to India."

vanilla beans

ginger root

nutmeg

peppers

Piñeda and the governor knew that a rich trade in spices awaited anyone who found a new route to India. They also knew that the king of Spain would reward them greatly if they found such a passage.

Governor Garay gave one other important mission to Captain Piñeda. "When you reach the city of Veracrúz, send word to Hernando Cortés that he is no longer the ruler of Mexico. The king has chosen me to govern the land. Even though Cortés is the one who conquered the land of Mexico from the Indians, he must now take orders from me."

Captain Piñeda promised to carry out the governor's commands. For many weeks his ships sailed closely to the shoreline of the Gulf of Mexico. On a piece of stiff parchment, he carefully drew the positions of rivers, bays, and islands. He made note of the kinds of plants that grew near the shore. Except for a few Indian camps, he did not see any large settlements of people along the barren coastline of the gulf.

More than three months later, the ships reached Veracrúz and dropped anchor at some distance from shore. Captain Piñeda chose three men for a landing

cinnamon

cloves

party. They were hoisted in a small boat over the side of the ship so they could row ashore.

"Look carefully at the land," said Captain Piñeda. "Find out if it is safe for all of us to go ashore."

A surprise awaited the three men in the boat. Hernando Cortés and his scouts had been informed of the approaching ships. With fifty soldiers, they had hidden in tall brush that grew near the shore. Cortés had no intention of allowing other Spaniards to come into his hard-won land. As conqueror of Mexico, he did not want to share any of the riches or glory he had gained. He intended to fight anyone who tried to take them away.

When Piñeda's men came ashore, Cortés seized them, dragged them into the high brush, and took their shirts, jackets, and caps from them. Disguising three of his own soldiers in the clothing, he ordered them to go to the water's edge and signal Piñeda to come to shore.

Back on board the ship, Captain Piñeda must have been suspicious when he saw the men waving to him in the distance. He told twelve more of his men to lower another boat into the water and proceed cautiously to land while he waited on the ship.

As they rowed close to the shore, four of the sailors, carrying crossbows and guns, jumped into the surf claiming the land for Governor Garay.

divider—measures distance on a map

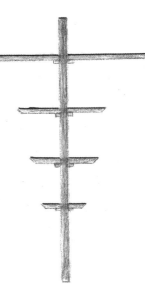

cross-staff—measures angle of the sun

3

Rushing from their hiding places, Cortés and his soldiers waded into the water, grabbed the men, and dragged them on to the beach. Seeing their friends taken captive, the remaining sailors turned their boat and hastily rowed back to the ship.

As soon as the men were safely on board, Captain Piñeda gave orders for all of his ships to pull up anchor and to set sail as fast as they could. He did not want to fight a battle with Cortés. He knew he could not win.

As quickly as the winds would carry them, the four ships sailed back up the coast of the gulf. However, their movements were greatly slowed by now. After so many weeks at sea, the hulls had become encrusted with heavy layers of barnacles. Sails had been ripped by the winds, and decks were rotting from dampness. The captain knew it would soon be time to stop for repairs.

At last, the ships reached the mouth of a great river, far away from the soldiers of Cortés. After anchoring by the river, Captain Piñeda himself rode in a small boat to shore. In keeping with the Spanish custom, he stepped into the surf, drew his sword to slash through the waves, and with great ceremony declared, "These waters and all this land now belong to His Majesty, the King of Spain."

Within a short time, the crews began to repair the ships. While they set to work, the captain chose several soldiers to explore the land along the river bed with him. During the next few weeks, they walked eighteen miles up the great river that was lined with tall palm trees. Piñeda named it "Rio de las Palmas" (River of the Palms).

Along the way, the Spaniards visited forty small Indian villages scattered near the river

barnacles

banks. They found the inhabitants friendly as well as curious. Never before had the Indians seen men with such light skins. They gazed in wonder at the Spaniards' heavy armor and metal helmets, their velvet coats with daggers in the wide belts, and the heavy flintlock muskets carried at their shoulders.

In turn, the Spaniards observed that the Indians' huts were made of mud and reeds, their clothing was of fringed animal skins trimmed with shells and feathers, and that they decorated themselves with tatoos and brightly painted designs. Although they could not speak the same language, the Indians and Spaniards exchanged bits of information by means of a hand-

sign language. Gifts were traded and the Spaniards parted in friendship from the native tribes before walking back to the mouth of the river.

It had taken forty days for the ships to be made seaworthy. Now they were ready for the voyage back to Jamaica. As Captain Piñeda and his crews sailed away from the river of tall palms, they may have admitted some disappointments. After all, they had not found treasures of gold or silver to take back home. No water passages to India had been sighted. Neither had Piñeda been able to claim all of the land of Mexico for Governor Garay as he had promised. However, the men had accomplished far more than they ever realized. They had made an excellent map of the Gulf of Mexico which would be useful to future explorers. They had found a great river which would someday be known as the Rio Grande. They had claimed the vast, beautiful country north of the river for Spain. And, they had become the first Europeans to set foot on the land which we now call TEXAS.

Route of
Alonso Piñeda
~1519~

NORTH AMERICA

ATLANTIC OCEAN

Rio Grande

Gulf of Mexico

CUBA

MEXICO

Mexico City

Veracruz

Jamaica

Caribbean Sea

PACIFIC OCEAN

CABEZA DE VACA
1490(?)-1555

In the country of Spain, the king anxiously awaited the arrival of a ship that would bring news of explorers he had sent to America. He had outfitted them with ships and supplies to search for gold and precious metals in the newly found land of Florida. Because great quantities of silver and gold had been found in the land of Mexico, the king was certain that more treasure would surely be discovered in Florida. He was in a hurry because he didn't want other European countries to get there before Spain did.

But the king had to wait more than seven years before he heard what happened to his band of explorers.

*sandglass—
measures time*

After leaving Spain in the year 1528, the king's ships had crossed the Atlantic Ocean and stopped in the West Indies where other Spaniards lived. Here, they gathered more men, horses, and supplies for their venture. Sailing in three ships, the Spaniards' next landing was on the western coast of Florida. For some months, they attempted to explore inland. But no matter where they went on the land, hostile Indians drove them out. Trying to escape, they hurried to the ships which were supposed to be waiting for them in the bay. But to their dismay, the ships were nowhere to be seen.

"There is only one thing to do," the men agreed. "We'll have to build our own boats so we can leave this dreadful place."

Although the Indians were harassing them all the while, the men built five crude, raft like barges. Cutting timbers near the shore, they lashed them together as planks. They filled the cracks with palmetto husks and smeared them with pine resin to make them waterproof. Killing their horses, they ate the meat and then melted down the horseshoe nails and stirrups in order to fashion tools from them. With the tail and mane hairs, they braided ropes to handle the sails of their rafts. Sails were shirts, capes, and breeches sewn together.

After filling horsehide "bottles" with fresh drinking

water, the Spaniards finally made their escape. With more than 300 men in five barges, they sailed to the west staying as close to the shoreline as possible. Although they did not know how far away it was, they hoped to reach the coastal settlement of Pánuco in Mexico.

"Our countrymen are the new rulers of Mexico. Surely we will be welcomed there," they reasoned. But the barges had traveled only part of the distance when a violent storm struck near the island now called Galveston.

In the lashings of the wind, the Spanish barges were torn apart, all belongings were washed away, and more than 200 men were lost in the high seas. Eighty survivors reached the shores of the island where they lay too weak and miserable to move. When 100 native red men suddenly appeared and towered above them,

the exhausted Spaniards knew that they did not have enough strength to defend themselves. To them, the Indians seemed like fierce giants who were carrying tall bows with strong arrows of cane. They were decorated with shell necklaces, tatoos, and pieces of cane stuck through the sides of their chests and lower lips. Their language was, of course, not familiar to the Spaniards but by using hand-signs, the men could partially understand each other.

To the amazement of the white men, the Indians knelt on the sand and wailed loudly for half an hour to express their grief for the destitute castaways. Then they disappeared into the canebreaks. The next day they returned with food offerings of fish and sweet roots. Bringing dried animal skins, they covered the shivering men. They also brought wood and built fires to give warmth to the Spaniards. Slowly, the shipwrecked men regained some of their strength. But they were still too weak to consider traveling onward, so they remained with their rescuers.

During the next few months, the Indians shared their meager food supplies with the men. But plants and fish were scarce in the winter season. Everyone, including the Indians, often went hungry. In desperation, four of the healthiest Spaniards with an Indian to guide them, left camp to search for a way to Pánuco.

"We will return with help soon," they promised.

However, they disappeared into the distance and were never seen again.

The remaining men suffered continuously from illness, starvation, and lack of clothing in the bitter weather. Most of them died and some were killed by the Indians. At last, only a few Spaniards were left. One of the survivors was a well-educated nobleman of Spain—ALVAR NUÑEZ CABEZA DE VACA (ahl-var noon-yez cah-bay-sa deh vah-cah). Cabeza had been appointed by the king to be treasurer for the Florida venture. Three other survivors were Lope de Oviédo, Andrés Dorantes, and Alonso Castillo. A fifth was a black man from Africa who was the slave of Dorantes. He was called Estéban, the Moor.

The Spaniards planned to stay together until they could make their way south to safety in Mexico. However, a sudden change in the attitude of the Indians delayed their plans. Believing that the white men would be of value to them as traders, healers, and servants, the Indians made slaves of them. They guarded them so closely that there was no chance for the Spaniards to escape.

When the Indians found that it was profitable to trade them to other tribes, the Spaniards were separated from one another. While some were kept on the mainland by their masters, Cabeza de Vaca and Oviédo were taken back to the island as slaves to a tribe of Karankawas (cah-rank-ah-wuz). During the winter months, they roamed over the island eating roots of underwater plants. Although he was ill, Cabeza was forced to gather the roots until his hands and feet were raw and bleeding from the sharp canes and spiny roots.

At night, Cabeza and Oviédo were beaten to stay awake in order to tend fires at campsites. Fires were necessary not only for warmth but also to ward off the hordes of mosquitos that pestered everyone constantly. Their lives became more tormented each day, but Cabeza kept the hope that he and Oviédo would find a way to escape.

During the months when it became impossible to find food on the island, the Indians took their captives along with them as they waded across the shallow bay waters to the mainland. There, by the bayside, oysters were plentiful for several months. During these times, the people ate well but, as usual, they were overwhelmed by huge swarms of mosquitos. Even though they smeared themselves with alligator grease and dirt to lessen the pain of the stings, their lives were hardly bearable.

Very little comfort was given by the shelters that the Indians built at each camping place. Set on top of small hills of shells called "middens", the huts were made of saplings which formed a simple frame.

Woven mats or
hides covered the frame
work. Because it didn't take long to build them, when
the camp was moved the huts were left behind. Only
the mats and hides were carried along to be used at the
next campsite. Since the Indians had no horses or
carts, all baggage had to be borne on the shoulders of
the travelers.

Because of the continuous hunger and ill treatment
by their Indian masters, Cabeza tried many times to
persuade Oviédo to flee from the island with him.
Each time, Oviédo refused.

"The Indians killed others who tried to leave," said
Oviédo. "I am afraid they will kill us too."

Finally, Cabeza succeeded in leaving the island all
by himself. Going into wooded areas on the mainland,

he joined a tribe of Charruco (chah-roo-co) Indians who treated him more kindly than the Karankawas had done. They allowed him to move freely along the coastal regions so that he could trade with their enemies and bring back articles of value to them. In his travels he went as far south as present-day Corpus Christi gathering seashells, cockles, and hard cane plants that could be used for arrow shafts.

With these things, Cabeza became a well-known trader among the scattered tribes. In exchange, they gave him deer hides, red dyes, flints, deer hair and tassels. His fame spread among distant tribes, especially after they heard that Cabeza seemed to be able to heal people of their illnesses with his prayers. From great distances, they came bringing ill family members. Once, Cabeza was so surrounded by the sick that he did not have time to eat for three days in a row. However, during months that followed, grateful patients often gave food and deer hides to him. Gradually, his life grew more bearable as he adjusted to the rigors of living in the wilderness.

During a period of almost five years, Cabeza roamed up and down the Texas coast, walking as far inland as 120 miles. He ate wild plants that he found and small animals that he could catch. In spite of extreme danger from wild animals, storms, cold, and hunger, he managed to survive. Each year he returned to the island to get his friend, but Oviédo would not consent to leave.

pecans

Sometime during the year 1532, Oviédo at last agreed to go with Cabeza. Wading to the mainland, the two men walked to the south and west to get away from coastal Indian tribes. Since Oviédo did not know how to swim, Cabeza carried him across four rivers along the way to a deep inlet. He called this wide bay "Espiritu Santo" (Holy Spirit). It is thought that this is the place now known as Matagorda Bay.

Joining another tribe, the two Spaniards went further inland to a stream which the Indians called the River of Nuts. (It was probably the lower Colorado River.) Of course, Cabeza and Oviédo did not know where they were and knew only Indian names for the rivers. Meeting with strange tribes who had also come to eat the plentiful pecans and walnuts, Oviédo became so frightened that he ran away to return to the coastal tribes that he knew. Cabeza was once more alone among Indians—a tribe of Guevenes (gway-veh-nez). He never saw Oviédo again.

walnuts

"Now," thought Cabeza, "I am the only one left from the shipwreck."

However, only two days later, Cabeza was told that some of his own people were with a tribe nearby. An Indian guide led him to a camp where he was united with Dorantes, Castillo, and Estéban. When they saw him, they were speechless with fright for they had been told that he was dead. Later, Cabeza wrote: "We gave many thanks at seeing ourselves together and this was a day to us of the greatest pleasure we had enjoyed in life."

While picking nuts to eat during the weeks that followed, the men met as often as possible. They recounted their adventures to one another, always expressing gratitude to God for their safety. They also made plans to escape but were careful to keep them a secret. They knew that the Indians did not want them to leave and that they might be killed if they were caught.

For six months they found no way to escape. They were taken further inland by the Indians into south-central Texas near present-day San Antonio. Here there was plenty of water to drink from clear streams and springs. And there were great meadows filled with ripe prickly-pear plants. All of the people gorged themselves on the ripe black and red fruit. When they ate all of the fruit in one field, they moved on to

another until the plants were stripped clean of fruit. But there were deer in this area too. With bow and arrow, the men shot deer to eat and made use of the deer hides for blankets and clothing.

Despite the plentiful food supply, the Spaniards still longed to find a way to Mexico. In October of 1534, commending themselves to God, the four men made their escape under the light of the moon. They were close to the headwaters of the Guadalupe River, perhaps near present-day Kerrville.

Hurrying to the northwest, the men walked through countrysides where many mesquite trees grew. Eating the mesquite beans and rabbits, squirrels, and small game animals, they seemed to have followed along the course of the Colorado River. As they went farther west, food became less plentiful. But the Spaniards were so accustomed to going hungry that they were able to stay well and strong with only a few mouthfuls of dried grass during a week's time.

After following the Colorado River for many days, the men turned off to the Concho River where it met the Colorado. Going directly west, they hoped to find food to be more plentiful. Seeing smoke from Indian lodges at one place, they went to it and met with a tribe of Avavares (ah-vah-var-ez) who received them in friendship.

For the next several months, the Spaniards roamed

mesquite beans

squirrel

rabbit

with the Avavares over Texas west to the Pecos River. With his skill in weaving mats and making bows and arrows and combs, Cabeza prospered as a trader. But food was so scarce, hunger was always with the travelers. Once, Cabeza traded nets and hides for two dogs which he and his friends ate to keep from starving.

Cabeza said it was cause for thanksgiving when the Indians gave him a deer or buffalo hide to scrape clean. By eating the fat next to the skin, he and his friends were sustained for many days. Such food appealed to them more than the spiders, ant eggs, crickets, lizards, earth, and wood that the Indians ate. Often, hunger even drove them to grind bones of fish and animals so they could eat the powder.

Coming to the edge of the Great Plains, the travelers sighted buffalo and hunted them down. A time of joyful feasting began, with Cabeza claiming that the

meat of the "hunched-back cow" was better than that of cows in Spain.

As word spread to other tribes about the ability of the Spaniards to make people well, the men began to be revered as gods wherever they went. Calling them "Children of the Sun," Indian scouts ran ahead of the men to tell others of the arrival of healers. Hundreds of Indians besieged the Spaniards, wanting to touch their clothing because they believed they would be made well if they did so. As many as 3000 to 4000 Indians followed the Spaniards wherever they went. Not any of them would eat or drink until the white men had blessed all food and water for them.

Adulation by the Indians grew even stronger after a successful operation was performed by Cabeza de

Vaca. Somewhere in West Texas, an Indian was brought to the Spaniards. He complained of pain from an arrow that had been embedded in his chest for a long time. With a sharpened stone, Cabeza cut deeply into the man's chest, removed the arrow, and then sewed up the gash with a thread pulled from a cactus plant. The success of the operation only brought more attention to the Spaniards. They were overwhelmed with gifts of food, hides, and shells—so numerous that they could not carry them all. By distributing everything among their followers, there was plenty for all and the journey continued slowly on to the west.

During the months that were passing, the Spaniards moved into an area of Southwest Texas that held the first farming Indians they had met. These tribes grew crops of beans and squash and they made bread from flour of the ground-up beans. Some even knew how to irrigate crops with river waters. When crops were poor, men of the tribes went into the mountains to hunt for deer and buffalo, bringing back the dried meat to their families.

With a great host of Indians following them, the Spaniards crossed the Rio Grande somewhere near the site of El Paso. This was the last time they were in the Texas area, for, as always, they kept walking to the south and west. Sometimes, for a short distance, their route went north to avoid mountains, arid places, or

gourd rattle—a present given to the Spaniards

hostile peoples. With friendly Indians to guide them, the Spaniards continued to walk on. For food, they existed on whatever the land and people could give to them even though it was often just a handful of straw.

After moving through lower New Mexico and Arizona, the men went directly south into the western part of Mexico. Following the Sonora River Valley, they camped near the village of Cumpas, where crowds of Indians gathered around them. Dorantes, who was able to cure many of those who were ill, was given the gift of 600 dried deer hearts. The Spaniards named the place Corozones (Town of Hearts). They distributed the deer hearts among the natives who were suffering great hunger because they had given all of their food supply to show gratitude to the healers.

Walking near the coast of the Gulf of California, the crowd of people crossed the Yaqui River in January of 1536. Still moving to the south for many weeks, they made an exciting discovery along the way. Castillo met an Indian who wore around his neck a small metal buckle with a horseshoe nail sewn onto it. The Indian said he had received this from strange men who rode horses and carried lances and swords.

"Only Spaniards have these things," said Cabeza. "This is proof that we are getting near to our country-men at last."

Hurrying ahead of the others, Cabeza and Estéban walked 300 miles further, following a trail of campfire ashes where the Spanish horsemen had stopped to rest.

Finally, near the town of Mocorito (mo-co-ree-toe), Cabeza and Estéban met four Spaniards on horseback. Because he was deeply browned by the sun and dressed as an Indian, the horsemen did not recognize Cabeza as a Spaniard until they heard him speak fluently in the Spanish language. At first, they were astonished at Cabeza's story of the shipwreck and listened intently as he told of his wanderings over the past seven years. But soon, they were taking more interest in the large number of Indians around Cabeza and Estéban. Cabeza saw that they would try to capture his Indian friends to make slaves of them. He begged the Indians to return north to their homes. Some of them did go back, but more than a thousand stayed because they believed they would be safe in the presence of Cabeza.

In the meantime, Estéban hurried back up the trail to tell the wonderful news to Castillo, Dorantes and their Indian followers. Several weeks later, he led all of them into Cabeza's camp. Then everyone proceeded with the Spanish soldiers to the town of Culiacán (coo-lee-ah-cahn) to meet with Melchior Díaz, the mayor.

After telling their story to Díaz, Cabeza and his friends were escorted to Mexico City. Here they were received with honor by the ruler, Viceroy Mendoza, during the month of July, 1536. To celebrate their survival through such a long and perilous journey, the viceroy entertained them with bull fights, great feasts, and festivals. He also had long talks with Cabeza and his three companions to ask them questions about the "new" land they had seen. As well as they could, Cabeza and his friends drew a map for the viceroy. It showed him how they had walked from the Gulf of Mexico to the Pacific during their seven years with the Indians.

Even though Cabeza told the viceroy that he had never actually seen any gold or silver, the viceroy asked him to make another trip to investigate the land more thoroughly. He was sure riches would be found.

"This time," declared the viceroy, "the king himself will give you plenty of horses, food, clothing, and supplies to take along for the expedition."

But by now, Cabeza had only one thought in mind.

"I want to go home to Spain," he said.

After resting several months in Mexico City, Cabeza sailed for home, arriving in Lisbon, Portugal, on August 9, 1537. Traveling on to Spain, he reported to the king who was overjoyed to see him and to hear the account of his journeys in America.

"Just think!" said the king. "You had not even intended to go there, but you found land that no one in our part of the world even knew was in existence!"

After spending many hours talking to the king, Cabeza wrote down the story of his wanderings as well as he could remember them. His book, *La Relación* (lah ray-lah-cee-own), was published in Spain in 1542. It was the first book ever written describing the land that was to become Texas.

Later, after going with an expedition into South America, Cabeza went back again to Spain where he died in 1566. He and his companions were to become known as the first non-Indians to cross Texas and the American Continent from east to west. They had seen people, plants, animals, and countrysides that no white man had ever seen before. And, as a result, many Europeans became determined to follow in Cabeza's footsteps.

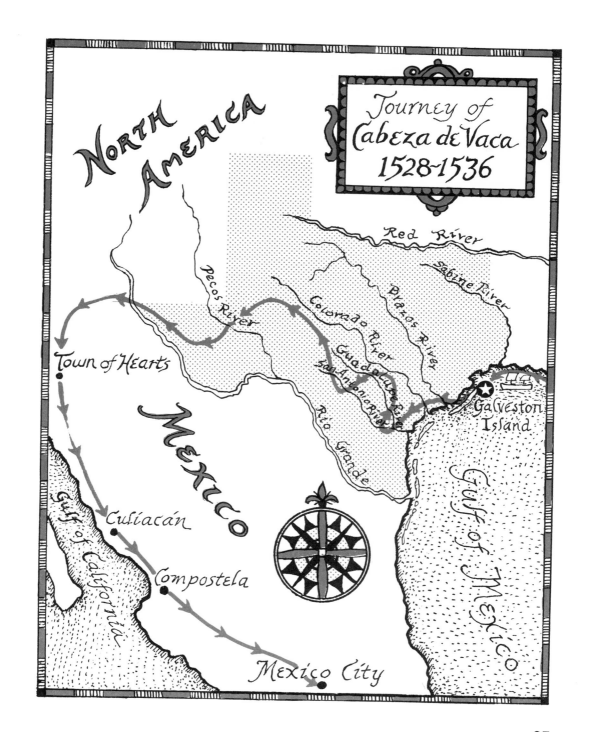

NORTH AMERICA

Journey of
Cabeza de Vaca
1528-1536

Red River

Sabine River

Pecos River

Brazos River

Colorado River

Guadalupe River

San Antonio River

Rio Grande

Town of Hearts

MEXICO

Galveston Island

Gulf of Mexico

Gulf of California

Culiacán

Compostela

Mexico City

FRANCISCO CORONADO
1510-1554

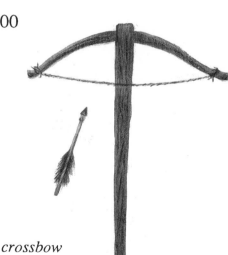

dagger

It was Sunday, February 22, in the year 1540. A grand parade was taking place in Compostela, a small town near the western coast of Mexico. Viceroy Mendoza, the powerful Spanish ruler of the country, had journeyed from Mexico City to watch the brilliant spectacle.

Leading the parade were 240 horsemen in shining armor. They were followed by sixty foot soldiers who wore helmets and padded jackets, pantaloons, and boots that reached above their knees. They carried the heavy weapons of their times—crossbows, harquebuses, shields, and swords. Next came 800

harquebus

crossbow

halberd

Indian allies armed with spears and bows. Then followed hundreds of Indian and Black servants. Some were leading the 1000 pack animals that carried supplies. Others were herding several thousand cows, sheep, goats, and pigs. These were to be used as food on the long journey of exploration to be undertaken by this great army of people.

At the head of the whole festive ceremony was a tall, fair-skinned young man whose golden armor and plumed helmet of gold glittered in the bright sunlight. Captain FRANCISCO CORONADO had been chosen by the viceroy to lead the expedition into lands that lay far to the north.

There were tantalizing rumors about this strange part of the world which was inhabited by native Indian tribes. It was said that in an area called Cíbolo there were seven great cities filled with gold, silver, and turquoises.

"If we can get to the Seven Cities of Gold before other Europeans hear about them, we can claim the rich treasures for ourselves and our king," Coronado said. And he had spent his own wealth to help finance the expedition.

Hardly anyone in Mexico doubted the truth of the Seven Cities of Gold, so it was an easy matter to find men to go with Coronado on his search. Eager volunteers had hurried to Compostela and now they were parading confidently before the viceroy in their fine array. They listened closely while he told them to obey their leaders. He promised that if they were successful, rich land grants in the new territory would be given to them. For such a reward, the men were more than willing to risk going into the unknown lands.

After the parade, Viceroy Mendoza journeyed back to his offices in Mexico City. Coronado and his troops left Compostela the next day to start the long trek to the north. There was only one man with them who had been north of the town of Culiacán, the outpost in northern Mexico. He was a priest—Fray (Friar) Marcos de Niza. In March of the previous year, Fray Marcos had been sent by the viceroy to establish a trail to Cíbolo for Coronado's army.

"Make peace with Indian tribes who may be encountered by our men," said the viceroy. "Also, take note of the rivers, trees, plants and animals. Examine stones and metals. Bring back samples of everything you can carry."

Leaving in March, 1539, Fray Marcos was accompanied by a small escort of Indians and soldiers. His guide was Estéban, the black man who had once crossed Texas and part of New Mexico on foot (see story of Cabeza de Vaca). Walking to the north, Fray Marcos sent Estéban ahead to

gather information from the natives. However, word soon came back to the Fray that Estéban had been killed by Indians who were angered when he entered their pueblo against their wishes.

In great fear, Fray Marcos hastily turned back to Mexico before he actually reached the Seven Cities of Gold.

"But I saw one of the cities in the distance across a very green valley," he declared to Coronado after his return.

"It looked larger than the city of Mexico and the streets are lined with shops of silversmiths and doors studded with turquoise. I was told that the women wore strings of gold beads and the men wore belts of gold."

Not everyone believed the fanciful tales of the friar. But Coronado chose to trust his words. So, he began the journey with Fray Marcos as the guide.

Coronado was also expecting the return of another small scouting party that had been asked by the viceroy to check the steps and the stories of Fray Marcos. This group was led by an old, trusted soldier—Melchior Díaz. He had fifteen mounted soldiers and some Indian servants in his command. Coronado thought that Díaz and his men would surely affirm what Fray Marcos had said and perhaps would bring back even better tidings.

So Coronado ordered his army to go on through the mountains and deserts of northern Mexico. However, before they had gone very far, difficulties arose. Horses and pack animals were exhausted by the heavy loads they had to carry. Much equipment had to be thrown by the wayside. Great numbers of cattle wandered off and had to be rounded up each day before the expedition could go forward. Progress was slow because only a few miles a day could be covered with such a large number of men and animals. A few of the travelers lost their enthusiasm and turned back home in disgust.

The men had gone 200 miles north of Compostela when more bad news met them. The scout, Melchior Díaz, stumbled into camp one day. He was ragged, exhausted, and deeply troubled.

"There are no signs of gold or jewels to be seen anywhere in the northern lands," Díaz reported, "and there are only a very few turquoise. What is worse, the Indians told me to bring word to you that they will kill any white men who come into their territory."

Although Coronado was dismayed by the news, he felt that he could not go back home until he had seen the Seven Cities for himself. He ordered his men to push on to the northeast, leading them into present-day Arizona. While crossing stretches of barren desert, men and animals became ill from clouds of dust stirred up by the hooves of the plodding horses and cattle. Since there was no grass and little water in the desert, many animals died of starvation and thirst. For 150 miles there were no villages or people to be seen, and the travelers were becoming more disheart-ened each day.

Having traveled 1000 miles from Compostela, the weary expedition came to the country of Cíbolo in May, 1540. In the distance they saw adobe houses built high up on terraces in steep cliffs. The only way to get to the houses was by means of ladders laid against the cliff walls.

This was the pueblo of Zuñi (zoon-yee) Indians. The Zuñis were not at all pleased to see the Spaniards coming and had lined themselves up at the base of the cliffs. When the Spaniards approached, the Zuñis shot

arrows and threw lances at them. But, frightened by
the guns of the Spaniards, they soon climbed up to
their houses and pulled the ladders up after them. Still
sending arrows, they also pushed heavy stones down
on the Spaniards who tried to climb the cliffs. Perhaps
because his golden armor shone so brightly, Coronado
was a perfect target. Wounded by an arrow and a
shower of stones, he fell unconscious to the ground.
But his comrades quickly dragged him to safety and
the battle continued.

After losing twenty of their men to the guns of the
Spaniards, the Zuñis asked for peace. When the fighting stopped, the starving soldiers immediately broke
into the storehouses of the pueblo and gorged themselves on the Indians' food supplies. But, thereafter,
they treated the Zuñis with kindness, giving them
presents of red caps, beads, and bells. They also made
the sign of the cross with their fingers or sticks of
wood trying to show the Indians that they meant to be
friends. It was an uneasy peace, but order was restored.

The Spaniards then took a closer look at the pueblo that was supposed to be one of the magnificent Cities of Gold. Pedro de Casteñeda, the scribe who kept track of daily events, wrote that it was "a little, crowded village, looking as if it had been crumbled all together."

Casteñeda also said that there were no silversmith shops, and that no turquoise or emeralds were decorating the doors as Fray Marcos had told them. In a wild fury, the disillusioned soldiers turned on the priest. Casteñeda wrote, "Such were the curses that some hurled at him, that I pray God may protect him from them."

Fearing the mood of his men, Coronado quickly sent soldiers to escort Fray Marcos back to Mexico. With them he sent a report to the viceroy. In it he wrote:

"I can assure you that in reality he has not told the truth in a single thing but everything is the opposite of what he related. The Seven Cities are seven little villages, all within a radius of 5 leagues." (15 miles)

After pacifying all the cities of Cíbola, the Spaniards continued feasting on the Indians' supplies of squash, maize, and turkey. At the same time, they listened to stories told by the Zuñis of a rich province to the northwest.

In late July, while he was still recovering from his injuries, Coronado sent out two

groups of explorers to see if they could locate this rich province. Under López de Cardenás, an escort of two dozen soldiers traveled twenty days to the northwest. To their amazement, they suddenly came upon an immense chasm with walls of rock. At the bottom was what looked like a narrow blue ribbon. It was the Colorado River of Arizona flowing through the great gorge of the Grand Canyon. Cardenás and his men were the first white men to see this astonishing sight. (No other white explorers came near it for the next 200 years.) But nowhere did they find any riches.

The second group of men, led by Captain Hernando de Alvarado, traveled into central New Mexico to a locale of twelve towns called Tiguex (near modern Albuquerque). The captain sent word back to Coronado that the friendly Indians at Tiguex had given food and clothing to his scouts. He also said that plenty of grassy land would make good grazing for the Spanish cattle. Alvarado added that the Indians told him of a very rich country that lay to the east. He suggested that Coronado bring the rest of the army to

Tiguex for the winter months to prepare for further exploration.

Impressed by such pleasant news, Coronado and his company were soon marching to join Alvarado. Once in Tiguex, they built corrals for the flocks, and set up tents for some of the servants and soldiers.

However, during the snowy, cold months spent at Tiguex, violent battles took place with the once-friendly natives. The Indians resisted the Spaniards when they arrogantly demanded houses, bedding, and food supplies that the Indians needed for their own families. After many weeks of bloodshed, the Spaniards subdued all of the towns of Tiguex. But they lost the friendship and trust of the chiefs and their embittered people.

While waiting for the wintry weather to subside, the restless Spaniards heard the tales of a Pawnee Indian who had been a captive of a nearby tribe. Because he looked like the Turks they had seen in Spain, they called him *El Turko*. Eagerly they listened to the Turk's stories about his homeland a long distance to the east. He claimed that near the Pawnee villages was a place that was filled with astonishing riches. It was known as Quivera.

"Even the common people eat their meals off silver plates and drink from golden bowls," the Turk declared. "Rivers are five miles wide and fish in the rivers are bigger than horses. The ruler himself is lulled to sleep by golden bells hanging from apple trees."

Once more Coronado's hopes soared. Perhaps the gold he sought just might be in Quivera. Plans were soon made to do further exploration.

By April 23, 1541, the army of soldiers and servants, horses, cattle, and pack mules, left Tiguex moving north along the Rio Grande. To keep track of the distance they would cover, Coronado assigned a foot soldier to count every step he took. With the Turk as their guide, they all headed for the Pecos River, crossed it, and continued directly east along the Canadian River.

Within two weeks, the travelers reached the Great Plains (also called Llano Estacado—meaning "Staked Plains") where numerous buffalo covered the flat land as far as the eye could see. The Spaniards were overwhelmed by the sight of what they called "horned oxen."

"I found so many cattle," Coronado later wrote, "that it would be impossible to estimate their number, for there was not a single day until my return that I lost sight of them."

Following the great buffalo herds were bands of Querechos Indians. These were nomads of the plains who did not farm or live in pueblos. Their shelters

were tepees that they carried along with them as they roamed the plains. Their homes, clothing, weapons, tools, and food all came from the buffalo.

With some Querechos and the Turk as guides, the expedition entered into the region of the Texas Panhandle. The flatness of the grassy prairie and the enormous expanse of sky was different from anything the Spaniards had ever seen. Since the grass sprang back up immediately after being trampled by the herds and army, there was no way to follow or establish a trail. Hunters lost their way in the great expanse because there were no trees, hills, or villages to be used as landmarks. Men back at the campsite built fires, blew horns, beat drums and fired muskets to help the hunters find the way to the camp. Some were lost for two or three days, some never returned.

Because of buffalo in this area, food was plentiful and there was grass for the cattle and horses. But Coronado was becoming uneasy about the direction the Turk was taking them. He was going southeast instead of northeast where Quivera was supposed to be. Although he had caught the Turk in several lies, Coronado still did not know that the Pawnee had plotted with resentful Tiguex chiefs to lead the Spaniards astray. The wily Turk hoped that a zig-zag course would confuse and weaken them so they would not be able to defend themselves against Indian attacks. Becoming increasingly suspicious, however, Coronado kept a close watch on the Turk as the journey progressed.

While moving slowly across the treeless flatlands, the company came upon a deep gorge in the terrain. Descending into it, they found a huge chasm with formations of many-colored layers of rock rising at the sides. A narrow stream ran through the floor of the gorge which later became known as Palo Duro Canyon.

Resting in one of the ravines, the Spaniards were extremely frightened by a storm of violent winds accompanied by hailstones "as big as bowls." Tents were torn apart, helmets and armor were dented, and many of the animals were injured. Except for three who were held by their masters, all of the horses stampeded. Only the natural "fencing" of the ravine slopes kept the horses from scattering over the plains. The terrified men cried and prayed. But, sometime after the storm had passed, friendly Indians brought presents of hides. The men soon forgot their fright and quarreled over the gifts!

Somewhere near the upper Brazos River, Tewa Indians visited the Spanish camp. Since they seemed to be trustworthy people, Coronado listened when they disputed the Turk's claim that he was leading them to Quivera.

"But Quivera is to the north," said the Tewas. "It is not in the direction the Turk is taking you."

With this warning, Coronado made some decisions quickly. First, he put the Turk in chains to make sure he went along on the rest of the journey to Quivera.

Then he chose thirty horsemen, six foot-soldiers, a priest, and a new guide named Isopete. He knew that he could move faster with a small escort instead of the whole company. Coronado then ordered the main army to return to Tiguex with the animals.

"Settle in Tiguex by the river," he told the soldiers. "Gather food for the winter while you wait for me to return."

Reluctantly, the main army made ready to go back to Tiguex. Hunters killed 500 buffalo to dry the meat in strips for jerky, a meat that did not spoil. There would be enough food for the whole trip.

Six Plains Indians went along as guides. Each morning they watched the sun rise in the East, turned, and shot an arrow to the West. Following its course, they would shoot another arrow when they found the previous one. Constantly keeping the correct direction in this way, they arrived in Tiguex on July 9, 1541. They had traveled 650 miles.

Meanwhile, Coronado and his men moved in the opposite direction across the Texas Panhandle. They followed the course of the Canadian River, camping at times in ravines that appeared in the table flat land. Except for the ravines and canyons, the land was barren, monotonous landscape to the travelers. Occasionally, Indian encampments were seen and the tribes presented Coronado with many buffalo robes as gifts. He carried them along to take back to Mexico as examples of the "horned oxen" that were unknown to people in Mexico.

After spending a month in the Panhandle of Texas, the Spaniards passed through more prairie lands in

southern Oklahoma and Kansas. Just below the bend in the Arkansas River on July 6, they came to the first settlement in Quivera. They found only grass huts and shy people who had very few possessions. In a letter to the King of Spain, Coronado wrote:

"Neither gold nor silver nor any trace of either was found among these people."

For twenty-five days Coronado and his men wandered through the meager villages of Quivera. In early August they came to the northern-most village of Tabas, in the central part of present-day Kansas. At this place, the inhabitants refused to give maize to the Spaniards' horses. Isopete, the guide, explained the reason to Coronado.

"The Turk is telling them to let your horses die from hunger. Then you and your men will not be able to defend yourselves and they will be able to kill you easily."

Coronado's anger flared. This time there was no reprieve for the Turk. Soldiers grabbed him and tortured him until he confessed. He admitted that there never had been any gold in the country of Quivera and that it had been his intention to lead the Spaniards out on the plains to "lose" them.

At this, the soldiers made a quick end to the Turk by choking him with a rope. After that, their only thought was to go back home to Mexico. They had had enough of fighting, hunger, cold, marching, and failure.

In late August, Coronado began the march back to meet the main army at Tiguex. He took the previous route across the Texas Panhandle but this time it was more direct. According to the stepcounting soldier, it was 340 miles shorter without the misguidance of the Turk!

Once back in Tiguex, the army settled down for the winter. It was here that Coronado met with a severe accident. The girth on his saddle broke while he was racing with a friend. As Coronado fell to the ground, his head was struck by the hoofs of his friend's horse. It took many months for Coronado to recover. But by the spring of 1542, Coronado was taking his people on the homeward path even though he had to be carried on a litter between two horses.

Two and a half years had passed since Coronado and his glorious army had departed from Compostela to search for the Seven Cities of Gold. After traveling more than 4000 miles, none of their hopes for riches and glory had come to pass. Of the 300 eager, proud soldiers, only 100 ragged, disconsolate men reached Mexico City in the summer of 1542. No one, least of all the viceroy, came to welcome them. They were considered failures by all their countrymen.

But in a letter to King Charles V of Spain, Coronado wrote: "I have done all I could."

His fortune, his reputation, and his health

spur

gone, Coronado died at age 44 and was buried in a Dominican cathedral in Mexico City.

It took many years for Spain to realize the magnitude of what had been done for the world as well as for Spain. Because of his tumultuous search, Coronado had opened the eyes of the world to vast, fertile territories that were unsettled. And for the Spanish Crown, he had claimed all the southwestern part of the American Continent with its wealth of possibilities for future generations.

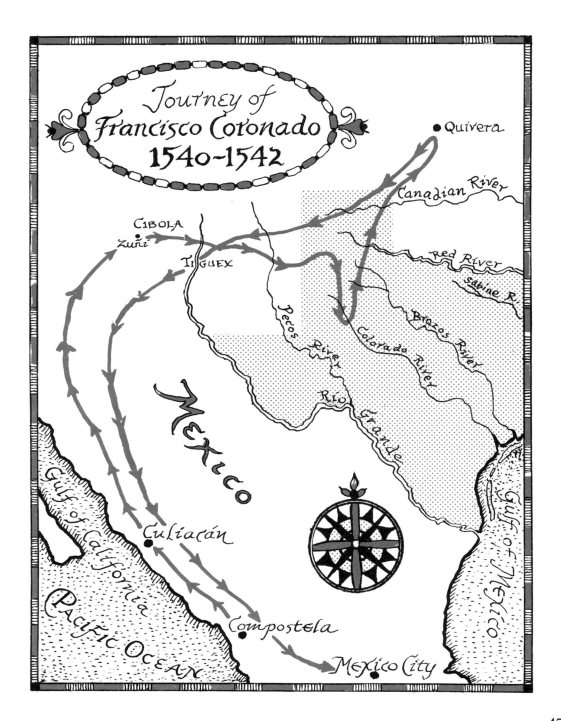

Journey of Francisco Coronado 1540-1542

Quivera

Canadian River

CIBOLA

Zuñi

TIGUEX

Red River

Sabine R.

Pecos River

Brazos River

Colorado River

Rio Grande

Mexico

Gulf of California

Culiacán

Pacific Ocean

Compostela

Gulf of Mexico

Mexico City

ROBERT LA SALLE
1643-1687

For a long time, Spain seemed to be the only European country interested in exploring the land of southwestern America. In northern America, the country of France was busy building up a fur trade with the Indians of Canada. England and other European countries were sending colonists to settle along the Atlantic seaboard of America. All of them were widely separated from the Spanish Southwest by a vast, unexplored wilderness. So it looked as though Spain did not need to worry about any other country coming into the territory that she had claimed for herself.

After Spanish explorer Francisco Coronado failed to find gold anywhere in the Southwest, the Spaniards lost interest in exploring. For more than a hundred years, the Indians north of the Rio Grande were left to themselves. They saw no white men at all, except for some horsemen who were slave hunters and a few lone missionaries. To avoid these intruders, the Indians quietly disappeared into obscure hiding places.

During this time, Spanish kings hoped that no one

would dispute their ownership of the immense, un-settled territory of Texas. For one thing, they did not have enough money to pay soldiers to defend it. It was taking all the gold and silver they could find in Mexican mines to finance their wars back in Europe. Besides, people who lived in Mexico did not want to go north to settle in Texas. They preferred to stay in their homes south of the Rio Grande where Indians were less hostile.

Unknown to the Spanish, however, were the dreams of conquest held by young ROBERT LA SALLE, a French explorer. La Salle, the well-educated son of a merchant in Rouen, France, had left his home in 1666. Following one of his brothers, a priest named Abbé Cavelier (ah-bay cah-vehl-yea), he had gone to Canada to seek his fortune. Although he did some farming on land granted to him at New Montreal, La Salle soon became more interested in the fur trade. The northern Indians, skillful in trap-ping fur-bearing animals, were willing to trade the furs for trinkets, blankets, cloth, and guns offered to them by the French. If the furs could be carried by ships to be sold in Europe, La Salle reasoned that great wealth would be possible for his country. But he saw that France would need a series of trading posts where the Indians could bring their goods. Also, seaports were necessary so that French ships could

pick up the furs and transport them across the Atlantic
Ocean to Europe. La Salle determined to make these
things possible.

During the next eighteen years, La Salle and his
companions endured great hardships, illnesses, and
disappointments. Yet, they built successful trading
posts and forts along the rivers in upper Illinois and
around the Great Lakes. French traders lived in the
trading posts. They bartered with Indians who brought
abundant supplies of the hides they had trapped. But
still they needed a seaport from which the furs and
hides could be transported all year round.

While working at the trading posts, La Salle listened with keen interest to stories that the Indians told
of large rivers that flowed in the west. One was especially long and wide, they said. They called it the

"Mesipi" (Mississippi) and declared that it flowed into the sea.

La Salle wondered where the river ended. He even wondered if it went to China! Eager to see for himself, La Salle traveled with several men to the Mississippi early in 1682. They paddled a bark canoe into the swift currents that carried them down the wide river. After two months, they reached the delta of the great river where three channels could be seen among small islands. There the fresh water of the river mingled with salt water of an immense gulf. La Salle and his friends were the first white men to discover that the Mississippi River emptied into the waters of the Gulf of Mexico.

After testing the depth of the water and exploring some of the surrounding land, La Salle determined that this would be an ideal place for France to establish a port. To lay claim to the area, he held a solemn ceremony with all of his men gathered. After blessings by the priests, the French flag and a tall wooden cross were raised. On the cross these words were carved in French: "Louis the Great, King of France and Navarre, reigns. The ninth of April, 1682."

The jubilant Frenchmen shouted as they threw their caps into the air, fired guns, and joyfully claimed that France now owned this river and the land around it.

They even said that France owned the land all the way to the River of Palms (the Rio Grande).

La Salle was already planning to go back to France to talk with Louis XIV. He felt certain that the king would finance the building of a port when he told him about the fine location that could easily be reached through the gulf waters. It did not seem to matter to La Salle that Spain had declared that no one but Spain could bring ships into the Gulf of Mexico.

Leaving seventeen men to build a small fort, La Salle started back up the river to Canada. All along the way he planted wooden crosses and laid claim to the fertile valley that was dotted with tributaries flowing into the great Mississippi. In honor of King Louis XIV, he gave the name of Louisiana to the entire Mississippi valley.

After returning to Canada, La Salle sailed for France. On arrival, he wrote a report of the explorations he had made in America and of all the forts he had built. He also wrote a summary of supplies he would need for more explorations. Only to the king himself did he intend to tell his plans for the future. Wisely, La Salle did not want to take a chance that Spain might hear about the plans. If it became known how close France would be to their borders in America, he knew that Spain would surely interfere.

In July, 1682, La Salle gained an audience with the

king. King Louis quickly became interested in La Salle's proposals. La Salle said:

"First, we will build a fort and colony where the Mississippi enters the Gulf. Our ships will pick up the furs that have been carried down the river and then take them to be sold in Europe. Because of the mild climate, the port can easily be reached at all times of the year by sailing across the Gulf from the Atlantic.

"Secondly, our priests can teach the Indians of the area to be Christians. Then they will surely be our allies. There will be at least 15,000 of them ready to help us fight Spain, for they do not like the way Spain tries to make slaves of their people.

"Thirdly, since we will have a strong garrison full of supplies at the delta, we will be close enough to Mexico to strike the Spanish both on land and by sea. A victorious France can then gain the wealth from the rich mines of Mexico."

It didn't take the king long to come to an agreement with La Salle. Not only did he desire to expand the fur trade, he also was eager to defeat Spain both in Europe and in America.

"I will see that you have 4 ships, 400 men, some cannon, and plenty of supplies," promised King Louis. "With these things, we can establish a supply base for ships and soldiers on the Gulf of Mexico. In time, France will become the strongest, wealthiest country in the world."

But neither the king nor La Salle knew what great hardships, mistakes, and disappointments were in store for their colonists and explorers.

On July 24, 1684, four ships left the French port of La Rochelle to head for the Gulf of Mexico and the Mississippi delta. They were heavily burdened with tools, provisions, weapons, and people. On board were 280 men with a few women and children who would be colonists. One hundred soldiers, thirty volunteers eager for adventure, servants, workmen, and seven friars and priests made up the rest of the passengers. One of the priests was La Salle's brother, Abbé Cavelier. Two nephews of La Salle were also members of the colonizers. A trusted friend, Henri Joutel, was to write of the events of the expedition.

Even before the ships left port, La Salle and the captain of the ships, Sieur de Beaujeu (suh deh bow-jeh) were quarreling with one another. La Salle was angry because he felt he should have complete charge of the expedition both on land and at sea. But the king had ordered that Captain Beaujeu should command the ships at sea and that La Salle would only direct the explorations on land. La Salle distrusted and resented Beaujeu even though the captain had had thirty years experience in the French Royal Navy. Beaujeu disliked La Salle because he seemed arrogant and seldom talked to anyone at all. The antagonism between these two men was to bring grief to everyone on the expedition.

Captain Beaujeu commanded from the *Joly*, the largest of the ships. It was filled with equipment, cannon, and baggage. A second ship, the *Belle*, was a small frigate which was a gift to La Salle from the king. The third vessel was the *St. Francois* (frahn-cwa), a small ketch laden with guns and supplies. *Amiable*, the fourth ship, held goods, tools, and pens of hogs and chickens for the settlement. In the cramped space left on the ships, the passengers settled in for the long voyage as best they could.

After three months of sailing, the ships reached the island of Santo Domingo in the West Indies on October 27, 1684. By this time, many of the passengers were ill. Although La Salle was very sick with a fever, he insisted that the ships stop at the island port to pick up more supplies. But during the night, Beaujeu deliberately sailed past the port and landed on the opposite side of the island. When the ships lost sight of each other in the dark, the *St. Francois* was captured by Spanish pirates. All of its precious supplies so necessary for building the colony were taken by the pirates.

La Salle and fifty other passengers who were ill, had to be taken ashore on the island. When he was told that the *St. Francois* was lost with all its valuable provisions, La Salle seemed to lose his sense of reason. No one thought he would recover. In anger and despair, many of the men of the expedition deserted, hoping to find a way back to France.

However, by late November, La Salle was well enough to continue the journey to the Mississippi. On the three remaining ships, the expedition proceeded to sail around Cuba into the Gulf of Mexico. They reached the shores of western Florida on December 28. From there, they sailed to the west across the gulf to look for the mouth of the great river. Staying close to the shoreline, the ships stopped now and then to get fresh water from streams that entered into the Gulf. On January 10, 1685, some of the seamen thought they had sighted the Mississippi Delta. But La Salle refused to land the colonists, and the ships sailed right past the river's mouth.

In defense of La Salle's decision, there were no maps to mark the delta. To make matters worse, fog often covered the coastal areas so that islands and channels could not be clearly seen.

More than likely, La Salle passed the river on purpose so that he could get closer to the Spanish land of Mexico. To this day, no one can be completely sure about his intentions.

During the month of February, the ships moved 400

miles further to the southwest along the shoreline of Texas. They often sent scouting parties ashore to explore, but each one returned saying they had not seen any signs of the Mississippi.

By this time, provisions were running low, and everyone was losing patience and courage. Captain Beaujeu and La Salle were in constant and violent opposition to each other. Beaujeu wished only to put the colonists ashore so that he could return with his ship to France.

At last, a large river that entered a bay was sighted on February 15, 1685. It is now known that the place was Matagorda Bay on the Texas coast and that the river was the Lavaca. But La Salle declared that the river was the Mississippi and ordered that everyone be put ashore. To guide the ships through dangerously shallow waters of the bay, the pilots put down a line of stakes to mark the safest pathway. Because he did not trust the capabilities of the captain of the *Amiable*, La Salle asked the pilot of the *Belle* to guide the *Amiable* into the landing place. But just at that time, word came that Indians had captured one of the Frenchmen who had gone ashore to chop wood. La Salle rushed to rescue him. While he was gone, the captain of the *Amiable*, disregarding orders, attempted to bring his ship in to a landing. Instead, he ran it into a sand bar and there it lay helplessly grounded.

When La Salle returned with the rescued Frenchman, he and his men hurried to save the guns, tools,
and utensils held by the floundering ship. They made
many trips carrying things in a small boat to shore, but
darkness overtook them before everything could be
salvaged.

During the night a storm arose. It dashed the *Amiable* and its remaining cargo to pieces. To make matters worse, curious Indians of the area stole some of
the things that had been saved from the wreck and ran
off leaving their canoes behind. The Frenchmen took
the Indian canoes for their own use. But that night the
Indians returned to get them and in anger killed two of
the guards and wounded two others. It looked as
though the 15,000 peaceful Indian allies promised by
La Salle had turned out to be 200 war-like enemies
instead.

As usual, Captain Beaujeu bickered with La Salle
about every decision that was made. He refused to
unload the cannon, iron, and ammunition meant for the
fort. He said that there wasn't enough time to do so
because the stormy season was coming and his ship
would be endangered. Beaujeu offered to take the *Joly*
to the island of Martinique to get more supplies for the
colony. La Salle refused his offer. So, taking along with
him some of the dissatisfied expedition leaders,
Beaujeu sailed away out of the bay. It was March 12,

1685. He never returned. Now, only the *Belle* remained of the four ships that had started out on the journey.

About 200 people were left with La Salle at the landing place. Most of them were ill with nausea and dysentery from drinking brackish water and having very little to eat. La Salle knew that he would have to find fresh water and a healthier spot for his people to live. Also, it would have to be a place easier to defend. Indians were finding it all too easy to harass the little fort and its occupants.

Of all the men who had journeyed with La Salle, the one he relied on most was Henri Joutel, the man who was keeping records of the events. He was a fair, reasonable man who respected his leader even though he did not always agree with him. La Salle knew that Joutel would care for the fort inhabitants wisely, so he left him in charge while he went to look for a better site.

With fifty men, La Salle walked five miles along the banks of the river to a waterway now known as Garcitas Creek. Here the men came upon a high bluff that was close to the clear water of the stream. Thousands of buffalo roamed in the area, so it would be possible to have a meat supply. At this favorable place, La Salle chose to build a permanent fort on the west bank of the creek. Going back to the temporary

fort, he ordered that everything be moved to the new
site.

In canoes which they built, the men carried the ship
timbers that had been saved from the wreck of the
Amiable. Precious supplies of remaining hogs, tur-
keys, chickens, and seeds were carefully transported
to the new place. Those men who were well enough to
work, built six small huts of saplings plastered with
mud. The roofs were of rawhides gained in trade with
the Indians. One large building had two stories. The

upper story served as a storehouse for food and weapons. The lower floor was a chapel and meeting place. One end of it held pens for the hogs and chickens.

At each of the four corners of a tall palisade that surrounded the compound, cannon were mounted. At one corner the flag of France flew above the walls.

The palisade also enclosed a large area for a garden

which was soon planted with wheat, corn, endive, and asparagus. Over the gate of entry was placed a wooden plank on which was carved the date 1684. La Salle named the place Fort St. Louis.

Great flocks of birds lived in the marsh between the palisades and the creek. Turtles and oysters were plentiful in certain seasons. Fish were abundant in the creek, and deer and small game animals could be hunted on the prairies nearby. Wild grapes grew in profusion and it seemed that food must have been plentiful. Even so, thirty people died while the fort was being built. Many others were ill. However, La Salle still clung to his secret hope of finding a way to get to the riches of Mexico.

By now, La Salle had admitted that the river where they had landed the ships was not the Mississippi. He told the colonists that he would leave to find it.

In October 1685, La Salle set out with sixty of his strongest men to hunt for the river and to explore the land. As before, he put Joutel in charge of the fort which now held only thirty-four men, women, and children. He ordered them not to let anyone come into the fort while he was gone unless the traveler could produce a letter of permission from La Salle himself. Especially, he warned them to be careful about dealing with Indians because they had proven so often to be untrustworthy.

With much anxiety, the little band of settlers watched their leader depart from Fort St. Louis. Even though he was a hard taskmaster, they knew that he was a courageous man and that he was their only hope of survival in this strange place.

With La Salle were his brother Abbé, the priest, and his two nephews. With the other men they walked down the river to the site of the original fort. For the next few weeks, they explored the bay area looking for the Mississippi River. It is thought by historians that the men then went inland to the west and south as far as the Rio Grande. No accurate records of this journey have been found but it is known that the French explorers met with Indians of the Rio Grande area. Although these tribes offered to join them in destroying Spanish outposts near the river, La Salle was not sure of their loyalty. Besides, he did not have

enough ammunition left for such an undertaking. His
men were weak and exhausted from the hardships of
the march through the wilderness. La Salle knew that
none of them were in any condition to fight well-
armed Spaniards. All that he could do was to study the
Spanish settlements along the Rio Grande.

Back at Fort St. Louis, the settlers worked their
gardens and hunted for food on the prairie each day.
Once, they saw a Spanish ship some distance out at
sea. They feared what might happen to them if their
fort would be discovered by the Spanish. But the crew

evidently did not see the fort for the ship passed on by.

Unexpectedly, the settlers at the fort received a bit of news about their commander. During one dark night, they heard a voice from outside the fort calling "Dominic! Dominic!" When Joutel made certain that the caller was one of their men who had gone with La Salle, he allowed him to come into the compound even though he carried no letter of permission. The man, Duhaut, who had been calling his brother Dominic, claimed that he had gotten lost from the other explorers and made his way back to the fort alone. He also reported that as far as he knew, La Salle and his men were all right. But he did not know where they were.

After an absence of almost six months, La Salle and his weary companions came back to Fort St. Louis in March, 1686. Their clothes were in tatters and their boots worn to shreds. They said little about where they had been.

As La Salle rested from the trip, he realized that the only way to get help for his people would be for him to go back up the Mississippi to Canada. As soon as he was able, he chose twenty men, including his two nephews and a friar to accompany him.

On April 22, 1686, priests said Mass in the chapel as all the inhabitants gathered around. After farewells,

the little band of men walked to the northeast over
rolling country to the open prairies where they saw
great herds of buffalo. Making a raft they crossed the
Colorado River. Then the San Bernardo River was
crossed near present-day Eagle Lake. Joutel wrote in
his journal that nineteen other streams were crossed
during the journey eastward.

Between the Trinity and the Neches Rivers, they
reached a place where many Indians lived. These were
friendly Caddo tribes who dwelt in houses of straw
that looked like beehives 40 to 50 feet high. The

Caddos owned horses obtained from their Comanche allies. It pleased the French that the Indians somehow had had contact with Christians and seemed to understand the sign of the cross.

While staying with the Caddos, La Salle and his nephew Moranget became ill with a fever. It was two months before they were well. During this time the other men explored land between the Trinity and Neches rivers, perhaps going as far as the Sabine River at the edge of Louisiana.

When La Salle recovered at the camp, he found that

the ammunition supply was so low that it would not be safe to continue the journey. Trading axes for five horses and some corn and beans from the Indians, the Frenchmen retraced their steps back to Fort St. Louis. When they reached the fort in August, 1686, there were only fourteen of them left. Four men had deserted along the way, one was lost, and one was eaten by an alligator.

The lonely settlers at the fort were glad to see La Salle and the provisions brought on the backs of the horses. Sadly, they told him that more of their people had died from malaria, smallpox, and Indian attacks. Of the original 180 people, there were now only forty-five left.

The colonists also reported another catastrophe. The *Belle* had been caught in a squall which caused the ship to lose its moorings. It was completely destroyed, and those on board were lost in the rough seas as they struggled to get to shore. Now La Salle realized just how desperate their situation was. Once again he made ready to go to Canada for help. The colonists helped him gather guns and provisions to go to the Mississippi. At Christmas, priests celebrated a midnight Mass in the chapel. Each person knelt at the altar for prayer, and many hymns were sung. Drinking a toast to the king with water from the creek, the men then loaded the five horses with provisions for the trip. Twelve of the most able-bodied men were chosen to go with La Salle. They started out on January 12, 1687.

For weeks the men walked in an easterly direction through rain-soaked meadows and forests. The way was difficult and tempers were becoming frayed. Surly and angry, the men fought over food and possessions. Several of them were openly hostile to La Salle, blaming him for all of their difficulties. Secretly, they plotted against him.

Near present-day Navasota (according to many historians), the men rested at camp. One day La Salle sent his nephew Moranget and several other men to find a supply of corn he had hidden on a previous trip. He stayed in camp with Joutel and the rest of the company.

During their search for the corn, the men shot a buffalo and cooked it over their campfire. But they quarreled over how the meat and bones were to be divided, some of them desiring the bone marrow as the choicest part. In anger, two of the men killed La Salle's nephew Moranget and two of his trusted friends as they slept. It was March 15, 1687.

As the hunters did not return to camp when he expected them, La Salle worried about their safety. With an Indian guide and Father Douay, a priest, La Salle set out to look for the missing men.

On March 20, 1687, La Salle and Fray Douay saw a man in the distance across a field of tall grass. Firing shots to let the man know of his presence, La Salle called to him as he walked on. Suddenly, shots rang out and La Salle fell to the ground. Two of his enemies (one was Duhaut, the man who had been allowed to enter the fort alone as he called to his brother Dominic) had hidden in the tall grass to waylay him. Because they knew that La Salle would be angry with them when he found that they had killed his nephew and two friends, they decided they would have to put an end to him too. They dragged his body into the bushes and soon left the place, disappearing into the wilderness.

La Salle had died instantly. With him went the dream of conquest that had lured the French to Texas.

Although La Salle's explorations in Texas seemed to end in failure, he is now known as the greatest of the early explorers in America. No one else matched his extraordinary exploits and discoveries. Because he led the way, the French people began the settling of Louisiana. They developed a thriving trade in the American Middle West and laid claim to part of Texas.

It was because of La Salle's entry into Texas that the Spanish were forced to realize they would have to take an interest in their land holdings. This led to their building of forts, missions, towns, and settlements in Texas.

AFTERWARDS

Under the excellent guidance of Henri Joutel, seven men (including La Salle's brother Abbé Cavelier) traveled up the Mississippi River and reached Canada. Several of them soon returned to France from Canada. For a time, the murderers of La Salle stayed in Texas with the Indians.

The people who had been left at Fort St. Louis did not fare so well. When the Spanish heard rumors of the French fort, they sent soldiers to search for it. After four tries, they found ruins of the fort in 1689. It had been laid to waste and the inhabitants killed by Karankawa Indians.

Later, it was found by other explorers that four of the French children had been kept by the Indians. One girl and her two brothers were ransomed by the Spanish and taken to live in Mexico.

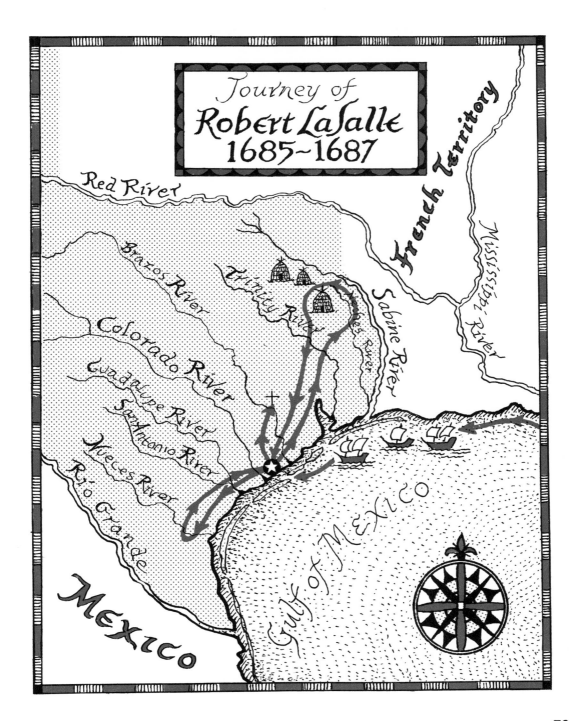

Journey of
Robert LaSalle
1685~1687

Red River

French Territory

Mississippi River

Brazos River

Trinity River

Sabine River

Colorado River

Guadalupe River

San Antonio River

Nueces River

Río Grande

MEXICO

Gulf of Mexico

74

DOMINGO TERÁN
(Dates Unknown)

Wild rumors flew across Mexico City in the month of September, 1685. It was said that large French armies were invading the territory of Texas. Some said that the French were on their way to capture towns along the Rio Grande because no one was there who could stop them. Perhaps all of Mexico was in danger of being overcome by the French. Who knew what might happen next?

Everyone in the city was aware that Viceroy Bucareli was questioning a group of pirates who had been captured from a ship in the Gulf of Mexico. Among the prisoners were several men who admitted that they had sailed with the French explorer, Robert La Salle. They insisted that they had deserted the French expedition in Santo Domingo and did not know what had happened to it. But they said they suspected that La Salle planned to build a settlement on the Texas coast so that he could spy on Spanish outposts at the Rio Grande.

"We don't know for sure, because La Salle never

powder horn

talked to us. He told his plans to no one, not even his own brother," the pirates said.

Spanish officials who were meeting in the viceroy's palace were thrown into a state of panic over the news of the French intruders. They quickly ordered a messenger to sail to Spain and ask the king what should be done.

"It may be many months before a message will get back to us from the king," declared the viceroy. "We must act immediately and send soldiers to search for the French Colony. All foreigners must be driven out from our lands."

As soon as he could, the viceroy sent a group of soldiers to hunt for the French along the Texas coast. The men were commanded by General Alonso de León and accompanied by several priests. During the next four years, De León and his company made four unsuccessful trips north of the Rio Grande hunting for La Salle's fort. At the same time, Spanish ships sailed along the coastline as the crews looked for the fort. Although they found remains of wrecked French ships, they did not locate La Salle's Colony.

At last, on April 22, 1689, General de León succeeded in finding the ruins of Fort St. Louis on Garcitas Creek (see La Salle story). He discovered that it had been destroyed by Karankawa Indians. Debris of broken bottles, torn books, shattered chairs and tables, and remains of three or four settlers and a few animals littered the desolate sight.

After burning the fort and burying the remains of the people, Padre Damién Massanet and the other priests with De León, held a religious service. Then the men searched the area for other signs of French settlers. But they found no traces of any foreigners at all.

Now, De León was no longer afraid of an invasion by La Salle. But he knew that other intruders would surely come because there were many French people settling in Louisiana—right next to Texas territory.

So the general held a consultation with Padre Massanet who was eager to teach Christianity to the Indian natives of Texas. Together, they made the decision to establish a mission before going back to Mexico to report to the viceroy.

On the banks of the Neches River (near present-day Nacogdoches), soldiers and priests built a small log building. Padre Massanet appointed several priests to remain at this mission which they called San Francisco de Los Tejas. (sahn frahn-cees-co deh los tay-hass). They were to begin teaching the natives to be farmers and Christians while he went back to Mexico City to ask the viceroy for help. As soon as possible, he would return with supplies to establish more missions in the same area.

When De León and Massanet reached Mexico City,

they found that word had come from the king of Spain. In his letter, he urged that the viceroy send supplies, soldiers, and craftsmen to build a total of eight missions in northeast Texas. Forts were to be constructed near the missions to keep the French and other aliens from entering Texas.

The king also gave a name to all the land above the Rio Grande. He called it the "Province of the Tejas" because of the large numbers of Tejas Indians located there. And he strongly urged that DOMINGO TERÁN be appointed as the first governor of the new province.

Domingo Terán, born in Spain, was held in high esteem by the Spanish king. He was a military man who had given twenty years of service in the Spanish-owned land of Peru. In 1680, he came to Veracrúz to be deputy of the consul of Sevilla and captain of the infantry. In a short time, Terán had made successful peace treaties with the Indians and also discovered a valuable silver mine. In 1686, he was made governor of two states in Mexico. Because of his distinguished past, the king reasoned that Terán would be a reliable leader for the expansion of Spanish settlement in Texas.

The king's wishes were followed and that is how Domingo Terán became the first governor of Texas. He hurried to Mexico City where he was given instructions for the expedition into the "Province of the Tejas."

He was:

1) to build eight missions among the Tejas and neighboring tribes
2) to keep a diary while exploring the land and rivers and learning about the natives
3) to make friends with the Tejas, entering their pueblos only if given permission by the inhabitants
4) to gather information about the French and other foreigners in the area, and to make prisoners of any outsiders
5) to find the most direct route to the mission on the Neches River, and to give names to rivers along the way.

Terán felt certain he could carry out the orders. But he was uneasy about the king's command that Padre Massanet should have charge of all supplies and enter into all decisions. Only military decisions would be left to Terán. Also, only fifty soldiers were allotted for the trip and he believed more would be needed.

However, Terán accepted the post. Gathering weapons, horses, and soldiers, he left Monclova, Mexico, on May 16, 1691. Traveling to the north, he reached the Sabinas River a few days later. Here Terán met with Padre Massanet, ten missionaries, and servants with large flocks of sheep, goats, and herds of cattle, mules, and horses. On May 26, 1691, the whole expedition headed north to the Rio Grande.

Reaching the great river, the expedition found a crossing place of shallow water about fifteen miles down the river from present-day Eagle Pass. The crossing was delayed when on the night of May 28 sixty-nine horses stampeded. It took four days to round them up but only twenty-three could be found. There was no time to look further for them because heavy rains were causing the river waters to rise rapidly. The small stock was not able to wade across the river and there was no wood available to make rafts to transport them. So the soldiers and priests swam their horses back and forth over the river carrying in their arms the sheep, goats, and chickens. It took five hours to move all the 1,700 animals across the river.

That night another storm raged for three hours. High winds blew down the camp tents. Trunks and belongings were so wet it took several days to dry things out. But once again, the expedition moved on to the northeast. Crossing the Hondo River on June 7, it met with Indians who became guides for the Spaniards

through the unknown land. Terán continued his practice of giving names to rivers and creeks that were crossed. The Hondo, he called "San Pedro" and the Nueces was the "San Diego." However, many of the old names remained in usage and most of the new ones given by Terán were soon forgotten.

Terán kept a written record of his progress and made maps of the route that he took. He called it "Trail of the Padres." Later, it became known as El Camino Real—The King's Road.

Traveling across prairie country, the men saw huge herds of buffalo, an animal unknown to them in Mexico. Progress slowed when dense thickets of mesquite and catclaw were encountered. With machetes the men cut a path through the tangled brush, and men and animals walked single file through it.

On June 13, 1691, Terán wrote that they had reached "a beauteous stream under a great stand of trees." He said of the place, "I named it San Antonio de Padua because we reached it on his day." (June 13 was the day celebrated by the padres in honor of St. Anthony of Padua, Italy.) This was the first naming of the site of the future city of San Antonio. It is also one of the few names given by Terán that has remained the same to this day.

A camp was set up by the stream and a celebration was held. Padre Massanet erected a large cross and

catclaw

built an altar under an arbor of cottonwood trees. All the padres held a solemn Mass for the company of travelers while curious Indians gathered to watch. Then the soldiers fired volleys from their guns and a feast was given.

After several days rest for the men and animals, the expedition moved on to the northeast. On June 19, it came to the Guadalupe River near present-day San Marcos. Camped at this place were five tribes of almost 2000 Indians. Because of the large gathering of warriors, Terán feared that they might be planning to attack his troops. He ordered his men to keep a close watch on their movements. Even so, the Indians managed to stampede the horses and to steal seventy-five of them. But they did not attack.

Among the Indians was a chief who carried two letters meant for Terán. The letters had been written by the missionaries who had remained at the Mission San Francisco de Los Tejas. They informed Terán that during an epidemic of smallpox, many Indians and one priest had died. Provisions were running low and the Indians were leaving the mission daily, stealing supplies and horses as they left. The situation was desperate, they said.

With this news, Padre Massanet became extremely anxious to move on as fast as possible to lend aid to the missionaries. But progress was slow because the smaller animals tired easily. Tension mounted between Terán and the padres.

After crossing the Guadalupe River, the company went to the Colorado River on June 26. Terán called it the San Pedro y San Pablo. The expedition crossed the Colorado about twelve miles south of the present site of the city of Austin. There they made camp to give a rest to the exhausted animals.

Because of the need for more supplies, Terán ordered Captain Francisco Martínez to take soldiers to Matagorda Bay. He had arranged for a ship sailing from Veracrúz to bring supplies for the land travelers. With 20 soldiers, 150 horses and 40 mules to bring back the hoped-for supplies, the men left camp.

On July 7, they came to the site of the old French fort near Matagorda Bay. For four or five days they explored the coast and looked for the ships. Others climbed the tallest trees to scan the horizon for sails. But none were to be seen.

While waiting, Captain Martínez heard that two young French boys were living with the Indians nearby. They were children who had survived the destruction of Fort St. Louis. The Spaniards per-suaded the Indians to give them the children so they could take them back to Mexico. They also gave a letter to the Indians to give to the ship's commander when he came. The letter would inform him that they had gone back to Terán's camp on the Colorado.

Captain Martínez and his company left the bay and got back to the camp on July 17 with their disappointing report. Terán and Massanet then discussed what should be done next. Terán wanted to send the men back to the coast again to wait for the supply ships because provisions were so very low. But Massanet wanted only to hurry on to the mission.

A vote was taken. Terán lost. He had to take up the march into East Texas. Although he left immediately, progress was painfully slow over the rough countryside. The padres became angry and impatient. At the Trinity River, without telling Terán, they hurried on ahead of the rest of the expedition. They got to the San Francisco mission safely and were met by the missionaries who cried with joy to see them.

General Terán could not quite understand why the padres went on without him and without the supplies so necessary to the expedition. All he could do was to follow them with his troops to the Tejas mission. On August 4, he camped near the mission and Indians soon came to meet with him. The general held a ceremony, appointing the Tejas chief as governor of the Indians and giving gifts to everyone present. His soldiers beat on drums, blew bugles, and fired six volleys from their guns. After this colorful display, they all marched to the mission where a High Mass was held by the padres.

Terán soon learned that the padres had founded another mission on the Neches about five miles east of San Francisco de Los Tejas. It was called Santissimo Nombre de Maria. The padres built it to have a place to nurse the Indians who were ill during the widespread epidemic. But the Indians blamed the padres for their sicknesses and became extremely hostile and rude. They refused to attend church services, and most of them left the mission stealing horses and corn as they went.

Terán stayed twenty days among the Tejas. Because food supplies were dangerously low, he decided to go to the coast in hopes of finding the supply ships from Veracrúz. Taking most of his men, he left the mission on August 24. He told the padres he would return to Mexico if the ships were not there.

At the site of the old French fort, Terán was happy to find two ships anchored in the bay. However, the

captain, Salinas Varona, had brought new orders for Terán from Mexico City. The viceroy ordered him to explore the country to the north before coming back to Mexico. This was bad news for Terán who wanted nothing more to do with the exploration of Texas. But he obeyed the instructions, starting out at the same time that one of the ships began its trip back to Veracrúz for more supplies.

In going north, Terán headed back for the missions with the new loads of provisions and gun powder. Violent rain storms fell all along the way. The countryside and rivers were flooded, making them all but impassable. Fog and rains made traveling hazardous and slow.

When the men finally arrived at the mission in late September, they found the padres living in constant fear. The Indians had made off with many cattle and horses. The chief who had once been friendly, told the Spaniards that he wanted them to leave immediately. Greatly discouraged, most of the padres said they were ready to leave and never return. But Terán persisted in doing further explorations as he had been ordered. In early November, he explored the area around the missions and tested the depth of the Neches River. He found that it would not be deep enough for ships to come into it.

With Padre Massanet and two other missionaries, he

went east to the Red River. Their horses were so worn out, the men had to walk. Many horses died in the freezing weather, and the men were miserable because they had no warm clothing.

But friendly Caddo Indians welcomed them into their pleasant villages near the Red River. For a week, Terán explored the area of the river and sounded its depths. It was found to be navigable for ships. But the Spaniards could not stay to build a mission because they had no supplies. They soon left the Caddo village promising the Indians they would come back as quickly as they could.

On December 5, 1691, the weary Spaniards began the trip back to Tejas country. Men and animals suffered from the severe cold. When almost all the horses died, the men walked the rest of the way.

After many hardships, Terán and his companions came to the Mission Santissimo Nombre de Maria on December 30. Anxious to leave the place, Terán planned to go back to the coast. But he had no horses or provisions for the trip. When he asked Padre Massanet for horses and supplies held by the mission, the padre refused to give them. He said the missionaries would starve without them.

The two men quarreled bitterly. Finally, Terán ordered his men to take some of the horses and cattle belonging to the mission. "I had to do this," he wrote in his diary, "because I ran out of supplies. It was winter and we had no food."

Six of the missionaries, discouraged about teaching the Indians either religion or farming, went along with Terán. Only Massanet and two other padres were left at the missions. Nine soldiers were assigned to stay as guards because the Indians were so threatening.

On January 9, 1692, Terán started for Matagorda Bay with his soldiers and the six missionaries. Again the march was slow and tedious over a flooded land that looked like a sea. It took three months before they arrived at their former camp on March 5. To their relief, however, Captain Barrota and his ship that held fresh supplies were there to greet them. With plenty to eat and warm clothes, the men regained their strength.

During this time, Terán stayed in camp for two weeks writing a report of his activities to take to the viceroy. He told about his frustrations with the poor planning that had resulted in such meager supplies for the expedition. He wrote about his displeasure with the padres who had refused to wait for the supply ships. When they insisted on going ahead to Tejas country without supplies, it had caused hardship and suffering for the whole company of men and animals. He described the insolence of the Indians and their resistance to religious training.

"The missions are useless," he declared as he ended his report. Wanting to return to Mexico, Terán appointed Captain Martínez to be in charge of the land soldiers. He told them to march back to Mexico as soon as the horses were rested enough to travel. Then

General Terán boarded one of the ships only to find that the captain had been told by the viceroy that they must explore the Mississippi River!

For a few days, the ship went along the coast to the north, heading for the Mississippi. But bad weather forced the men to turn back. Much to Terán's relief, the ship sailed for Veracrúz, arriving on April 15, 1692.

Domingo Terán's exploring days were over, seemingly a failure. The expectation of founding more missions had not been fulfilled. There was little hope that the two missions left in Tejas country would be able to survive much longer. The land, rivers, and hostile Indians seemed to hold no promise for the Spanish plans to settle the Province of Tejas.

Perhaps the most lasting thing that came from Terán's trip was the establishing of El Camino Real— the road that he laid out from Monclova to Louisiana. Today, more than 300 years later, Highway 21 is essentially the same route take by Terán. Every five miles a large stone monument marks the road. On each one is a bronze plaque describing the work of the explorers.

Because of Terán's efforts, Texas still has El Camino Real—the first planned road in all of America.

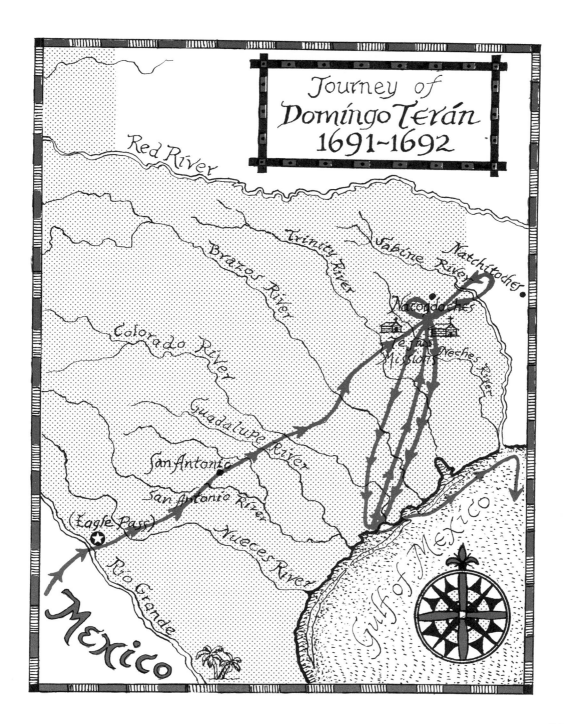

Journey of Domingo Terán 1691–1692

Red River

Trinity River

Sabine River

Natchitoches

Brazos River

Nacogdoches

Colorado River

Tejas Missions

Neches River

Guadalupe River

San Antonio

San Antonio River

(Eagle Pass)

Nueces River

Rio Grande

MEXICO

Gulf of Mexico

ATHANASE DE MÉZIÈRES
1715 - 1779

When young ATHANASE de MÉZIÈRES (ah-teh-naze deh may-zee-air) was a schoolboy in Paris, France, it was not likely that he ever dreamed of fighting Indians in Texas or sitting by a campfire to smoke a pipe of peace. After all, his mother and father were aristocrats with close ties to the king of France. They sent Athanase to the finest schools where he excelled in mathematics and learned to write fluently in both French and Latin. His world was far removed from the untamed wilderness of America.

Since Athanase was such a fine scholar, his parents might have expected him to gain prestige and royal favor when he became a man. Perhaps he would even

peace pipe

be honored throughout France. But such dreams vanished when Athanase de Mézières was eighteen years old. Leaving France and his school days behind, he sailed for America in 1733.

The ship that carried Mézières to the New World landed at the port of New Orleans on the Gulf of Mexico. Situated in the Louisiana Territory, New Orleans had been founded by the French only fifteen years earlier. But it was already a place that bustled with activity. Crowds of Indians, traders, and frontiersmen mingled as they gathered at the docks to watch the arrival of French ships which were laden with cargos of guns, gun powder, barrels, and other European products. The ships were bringing these goods to be bartered in exchange for American furs and hides which could be sold for high prices in Europe. It was a time of great opportunity for anyone in Louisiana who would brave the dangers of frontier living to gather furs and deer hides from the Indian hunters.

Even though there were far more Indians than French settlers living in the Louisiana Territory, Mézières soon felt right at home among the small groups of his countrymen. He bought a plantation where, with the help of thirty-five slaves, he raised tobacco, maize, and a variety of grains. Like the other French planters, he was also a soldier. Stationed at the

maize

tobacco leaves drying

military post of Natchitoches (nack-eh-tush) in north-western Louisiana, he took part in battles against hostile Indians, especially tribes of Comanches and Lipan Apaches.

Because of his skill as a fighter and his ability to live in the wilderness by learning the ways of the Indians, Mézières came to the attention of the French military authorities. They gave him frequent promotions and often chose him to carry out difficult assignments in the territory.

After 1743, Mézières spent most of his time at the post of Natchitoches which was located within a few miles of the Territory of Texas in the Red River Valley. As a successful trader with friendly Indian tribes,

*bear fat, gun,
and red cap*

he became familiar with their customs and learned to
speak several of their languages. He relied on them
for supplies of furs, horses, and bear fat and gave
them guns, ammunition, and tobacco in return.

When his trading business prospered, Mézières
married a young French woman. She died two years
later, leaving one daughter. He and his second wife
raised a large family of children while they lived in
Natchitoches. All the while, Mézières was becoming
more and more involved in the activities and problems
of frontier life. Traveling throughout the area, he
gained a broad knowledge of the land and the needs of
its people.

Mézières knew that one of the foremost problems in
this part of Louisiana was the uncertainty of land
ownership. The Territory of Texas joined Louisiana

somewhere near the Sabine River. But no one was sure just where the boundary line should be. It had never been surveyed or mapped. When the Spanish built a fort, the presidio of San Agustín, on the Trinity River, the French believed it was on *their* land. Because he thought it was questionable, the French governor of Louisiana wrote a letter to Spanish officials who lived nearby in the small settlement of Los Adaes (lohs ah-die-ace). He asked Mézières to be his agent.

"Carry this letter to the Spaniards," the governor said. "Ask them to meet with us so that decisions can be made about where the boundary line should be."

Mézières made the trip to Los Adaes in 1756 but the Spanish refused to discuss the matter. He went home without an answer, but Mézières knew that the question would come up again as more and more settlers came to live in the area.

Although the Spaniards would not talk about the borderline, they were extremely uneasy about the closeness of the two countries. They did not have the soldiers or the funds to protect their land from the French or anyone else who came into Texas. The few small missions and presidios which they maintained for the Indians were not successful. The Indians did not want to stay in the missions. They stole horses and supplies as they left to go back into the wilderness. So

the Spanish knew they could not expect the Indians to help in protecting the borderlands.

Further cause for alarm among the Spaniards was that there were other intruders besides the French. English ships were sailing along the shoreline of Texas bringing guns, barrels, rum, beef, horses, and sugar for the Indians to buy. The English were also entering Texas from the north through Arkansas to sell guns to tribes who hated the Spanish and French. The situation was becoming more and more tense because neither the French nor the Spanish wanted English people in their lands. As for the majority of Indians, they seemed to prefer whoever gave them the goods that they wanted.

The tension was lessened by a rather unexpected chain of events that happened in Europe. After many years of battling England and Spain, France had to admit defeat. Drained of its wealth, it could no long take care of its land holdings in America. Rather than give them to England, France ceded its lands to Spain in the year 1762. The French Territory of Louisiana then became part of Spain. All of its people were considered to be Spanish citizens. A Spanish governor was appointed for Louisiana with New Orleans as the headquarters for the new government.

By 1763, Mézières and all the other French soldiers had been discharged from the French military service and made part of the Spanish militia. As a Spanish soldier, Mézières stayed at his post in Natchitoches to serve his new country.

At first, some of the officials were not sure they could trust a Frenchman to be a loyal citizen of Spain. They tried to find fault with Mézières but, even though he made some mistakes, he soon won their trust. He helped them find capable Frenchmen to hold minor offices in the new government. He put unlicensed traders out of business and chased outlaws away from Natchitoches. Then he set up ways to police northwestern Louisiana. He spent his own money to repair government buildings and raised money to rebuild the town church.

It wasn't long before the Spaniards asked Mézières to explore the land and to visit native tribes of the northern frontier. They believed that he was the ideal man to win the loyalty of the Indians to Spanish rule because he had known them well for such a long time. Besides, he had learned to live in the wilderness and to find his way in unmapped regions.

On the other hand, Mézières knew that it was important for the Spanish to be friends with the Indians. Not only did they want their trade, but they also needed friendly tribes to help keep the warring Apaches and Comanches out of Texas. Horse stealing and raids by these tribes were constant threats to all of the settlers on the northern frontier.

Traveling to the camps of Wichita and Caddo tribes, Mézières smoked the peace pipe with them.

"We are now all Spaniards," he told them. "We must learn to get along together and support the Spanish government."

To keep their goodwill, Mézières hoped to continue the French practice of selling guns to the Indians. But some of the Spanish officials did not feel that it was safe to give guns and ammunition to Indians, friendly or not.

"If we give guns to them, they will fight against us and not become part of our country," declared the officials.

In 1767, the governor decided to forbid trading with

the Indians in northeast Texas. His edict made them very angry.

"We will starve to death if we don't have guns for hunting for our food," they said.

Fortunately for the Indians, Mézières was appointed as the governor of Natchitoches in 1769. He convinced the Spanish to change their minds.

"If you do not give guns to them, the Indians will turn to the English for their supplies," he told the governor of Texas. "Spain will completely lose the loyalty of all the Indians."

medal

The Spanish governor agreed with Mézières. He asked him to go as an ambassador of peace to villages in Northeast Texas. In April of 1770, Mézières visited Caddo and Wichita bands on the Red River. He brought many gifts of beads, knives, axes, balls, cloth, and other things they liked. He talked with the chiefs and told them that the Spanish were willing to send traders to their villages again. Appointing tribal chiefs as captains, he presented them with medals to wear and flags to carry. Pleased with these marks of prestige and honor and with the promise of gun supplies, the chiefs agreed not to trade with Englishmen who

Indian "ball"

came to their camps. They gave their lands to the king of Spain and said they would work for peace among Nations of the North. They also promised that they would go to San Antonio and sign a treaty with the governor of Texas.

During the same year, Mézières sold his plantation to pay debts that had mounted during his frequent absences. Also, in his office as governor of Natchitoches, he wanted to spend more time trying to solve the problems of the Louisiana-Texas borderlands.

By 1771, Mézières had won the friendship of bands who had once been allies with the dreaded Comanches. Soldiers with Mézières said, "These Indians are making promises to buy guns only from us. They say they will help us fight the Apaches and Comanches. But they won't keep their promises."

In answer, Mézières said, "Let's give them a chance." He even sent gifts and messages of peace to Comanche enemies. They kept the gifts but they refused to meet with him.

Nevertheless, Mézières continued to work as a peacemaker. In 1771, six tribes signed treaties with him. Four of the chiefs, to show they meant to maintain harmony, wrapped themselves in one large Spanish flag.

The Spanish were finding that Mézières was invaluable to them as an explorer as well as a peacemaker.

His reports were more precise than any they had ever received about the people and lands of the Texas-Louisiana borderlands. During his travels, he took a census of the numbers of people living in Northeast Texas. He made detailed maps as he explored the land and rivers, sending accurate geographical reports to Governor Rippardá in San Antonio. He wrote that the fertile soil and amounts of rainfall would be excellent for growing crops which would attract farmers to the area. In visiting Spanish missions which were struggling to survive, he found that the priests were discouraged about taking care of their property and their unwilling Indian converts. To the viceroy in Mexico City, Mézières reported all these things in detailed, well-written letters.

In early 1772, Mézières traveled again among the Indian nations who lived along the Brazos River. Riding with him were eight Frenchmen and one Spaniard from Los Adaes. Going to the west, they crossed the Sabine, Angelina, Neches, and Trinity rivers. At the future site of Waco near the Brazos, they met with bands of Tonkawa Indians and gained their friendship while learning their customs and studying the possibilities of the land.

Going up the Brazos River 200 miles further, Mézières reached the Red River in March, 1772. He was joyfully greeted by friendly Wichitas who had remained faithful to the treaties they had made earlier. When they told him they needed help to fight marauding Apaches, Mézières promised he would ask the governor for soldiers and equipment for them.

Having signed treaties with nine tribes, he rode south 400 miles to San Antonio in company with seventy Indians. In the San Antonio plaza they met with the governor to declare loyalty to Spain. As a symbol of their friendship, the Indian chiefs buried a hatchet and performed a feather dance, afterwards presenting a gift of the feathers to the governor.

By July, 1772, Mézières was back in Natchitoches

hatchet

where he had been advanced to the rank of lieutenant colonel in recognition of his services to Spain. Needing to settle some business in his homeland, he left for France in April of 1773. During the next nine months, he visited with family members, attended to business affairs, and was received with honor by the kings at the courts of France and Spain. At least part of the dreams his parents once held had come true after all.

While Mézières was gone, the Spanish viceroy decreed that the missions in Northeast Texas would be closed. He ordered all Spanish settlers in that region to move to San Antonio. The missions of Bahia and San Antonio were the only places of Spanish influence left north of the Rio Grande. In all, there were scarcely 3000 people living in the Territory of Texas.

Families from East Texas were reluctant to leave the homes and ranches they had worked so hard to build. Although they moved to San Antonio, they did not like the climate, the poor soil, and the frequent raids from Comanche bands. After a short while, a group of them went back to East Texas under the leadership of Gil Ybarbo, a successful trader and rancher. They established the settlement of Bucareli on the Trinity River in 1774 even though they had no permission from the governor to do so.

In February of 1774, Mézières returned from Europe and arrived in Natchitoches in March. He went to work immediately, receiving visits from friendly chiefs who desired more traders to come to their villages.

Asked by the governor to explore East Texas to find out about the loyalty of Indians there, he traveled to the south of Natchitoches. After months of observing the Indians along the coast and further into the interior, he sent a report to the governor. Of each group of tribes, he said:

1) The primitive coastal Indians should be overlooked because they would not be of help in developing the civilization of Texas.
2) All Tejas Indians in East Texas were friendly but they were not interested in helping Spain destroy Comanches and Apaches because they did not like to go to war.
3) Although many of the Nations of the North were warlike, only the Comanches and Apaches were still hostile to Spain.

Mézières recommended that war be carried on against enemy tribes. However, plans for a war had to be set aside because a deadly epidemic ran through the Louisiana-Texas regions in 1777. Many Indian tribes were entirely wiped out because of disease. Among the numerous deaths in Natchitoches, those of Mézières' wife and two of his children occurred in the same week. He set about to raise the rest of his children alone. Taking four of his sons with him on his travels whenever he could, he arranged for some of the other children to be sent to boarding schools while he went back to his work as an ambassador for the Spanish.

In February 1778, Mézières was called to San Antonio to make plans to fight the Apaches. Governor Ripparda asked him to talk to Tonkawa and Wichita tribes on the Upper Red River to see if they would join in warfare. In March, Mézières left the city with twenty-two soldiers from the San Antonio garrison, six militiamen from Natchitoches, and two of his sons. After meeting with tribes of Kichais, Tonkawas, and Tawakanis, he continued north to the Red River along the edge of the Cross Timbers. In each area, he gained tribal support for warring against the Apaches. Going through rugged, untracked regions, he looked for camps of the Comanches, hoping to talk peace with them. Although he found their corrals and camp-sites, he did not find the people.

During this time, he was writing letters, sixteen in all, of his observations and descriptions of the land as he and his companions crossed the Guadalupe, Colorado, and Brazos rivers. He emphasized the beauties of the land and its favorable conditions that would attract new settlers.

In March of 1779, Mézières was in New Orleans to plan another expedition to Nations of the North to proclaim the goodwill of Spain. He hoped to mend rifts between tribes, to persuade runaways from the missions to return, and to get the Tonkawas to settle down in villages to be farmers.

On May 24, he left Natchitoches with twenty-seven soldiers and sixteen civilians. They intended to visit the new settlement of Nacogdoches which had been founded by Gil Ybarbo close by the Sabine. At the Atoyaque River, a messenger brought word that the settlement had been attacked by Comanches. In hurrying to go to its aid, Mézières fell from his horse and was badly injured. Instructing his men to remain at a camp by the river, he was then carried on a stretcher between two horses all the way back to his home in Natchitoches.

For three months, Mézières lay ill, all the while worrying about neglecting the Indians of the interior. Before he was fully recovered, he went back to the Atoyaque River and joined his men to continue the expedition. After visits with Tonkawa and Tejas tribes, he went to San Antonio to meet with chiefs there. His hope was to get them to make peace with the Comanches and to convince them to be farmers instead of roving hunters. To aid his cause, he carried presents of hatchets, spades, guns and gun powder,

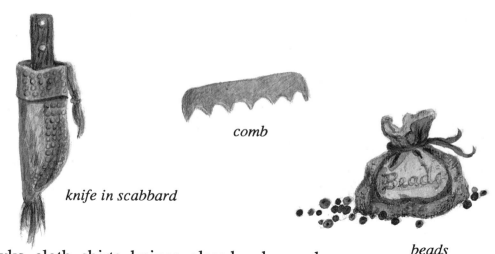

knife in scabbard

comb

beads

tomahawks, cloth, shirts, knives, glass beads, combs, and tobacco.

Mézières was not happy to find that he had been appointed by the king to be governor of Texas with offices in San Antonio. He preferred the work of trying to bring harmony between all of the people in Northeast Texas and he did not want to leave his home in Natchitoches.

spade

But Mézières did not live long enough to take office as the governor of Texas. With complications resulting from his fall, he became seriously ill in San Antonio. Realizing he did not have long to live, he wrote to a friend asking him to care for his young children. He died on November 1, 1779, and was buried with military honors in the parish church of the Villa de San Fernando.

In his lifetime, Mézières had proven to be an exceptionally skillful explorer and peacemaker. With his explorations of Central and Northeast Texas, he had

Governor's palace in San Antonio

provided Spain with the most valuable information it had ever received from the Province of Texas. He had steered Spain through difficult decisions and managed to keep peace between the Indian, French, and Spanish peoples.

With the work of Athanase de Mézières, the last major exploration of Texas had been completed.

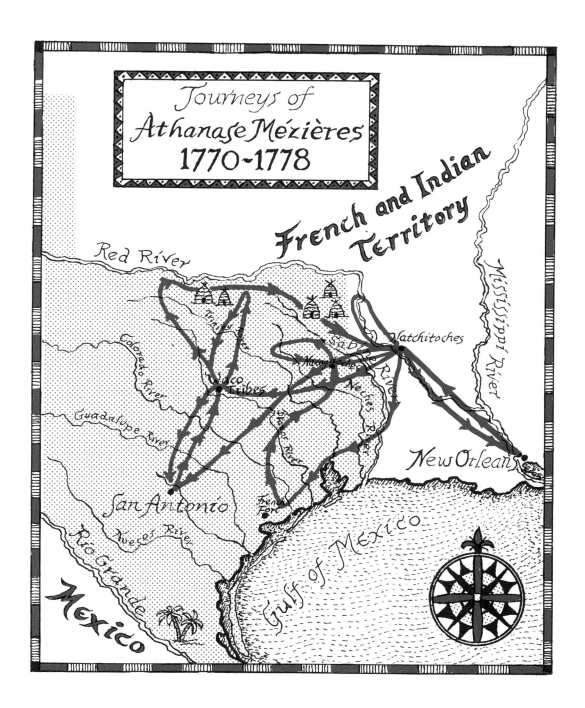

Journeys of
Athanase Mézières
1770~1778

French and Indian Territory

Red River

Mississippi River

Natchitoches

Sabine River

Massanet

Waco Tribes

Colorado River

Neches River

Guadalupe River

Brazos River

New Orleans

San Antonio

French Fort

Nueces River

Rio Grande

Gulf of Mexico

Mexico

WHEN THE EXPLORATIONS TOOK PLACE

1519	**ALONSO PIÑEDA** explores land at mouth of Rio Grande.
1520	DIEGO CAMARGO tries to build a fort at the Rio Grande but is chased out by the Indians.
1523	FRANCISCO GARAY, planning to build a fort at the mouth of the Rio Grande, is captured by Cortés.
1528	**CABEZA de VACA**, after being shipwrecked, walks over south-central Texas with various Indian tribes.
1542	LUÍS MOSCOSO and soldiers explore northeast Texas after reaching the Red River from the east.
1542	**FRANCISCO CORONADO** crosses the Panhandle of Texas.
1553	Friar de MENA walks over the lower coastal area after being shipwrecked.
1568	Their ship destroyed by the Spanish, 3 ENGLISH SAILORS walk the entire Texas coastline to the north and return to England.
1579	HERNAN GALLÉGOS with FRANCISCO CHAMUSCADO explores the Rio Grande in West Texas, finds the junction of Rio Concho and the Rio Grande, and goes to the headwaters of the Canadian River.
1582	ANTONIO de ESPÉJO finances his own expedition to explore the Pecos River.
1583	DIEGO PERÉZ de LUXÁN explores the southwest.

1590	GASPAR de SOSA follows the Rio Grande and Pecos River to the Davis Mountains.
1593	FRANCISCO BONILLA, JUAN de HUMANA, and Indian guide, JUSEPHE, go north from El Paso over the Great Plains to Quivera.
1598	JUAN de OÑATE crosses the Texas Panhandle to go to the Province of Quivera.
1638	JACINTO de SEPULVEDA follows the Rio Grande east to the Gulf of Mexico.
1650	DIEGO del CASTILLO finds pearls in the Concho River while exploring North Central Texas.
1654	DIEGO de GUADALAHARA leads an expedition to the Concho River regions.
1682	ANTONIO de OTERMÍN establishes the mission of Ysleta at the future site of El Paso.
1685	**ROBERT la SALLE**, a Frenchman, builds a fort on Matagorda Bay and explores to the northeast and south to the Rio Grande.
1686	ALONSO de LEÓN explores coastal areas looking for the French fort built by La Salle.
1691	**DOMINGO TERÁN** crosses Texas from the Eagle Pass area to the Louisiana border, establishing El Camino Real, the first planned road in Texas.

1716	Friar ANTONIO MARGIL establishes 6 missions near the Louisiana border.
1718	MARTIN de ALARCÓN and ANTONIO de OLIVARES establishes the settlement of San Antonio (called Bexár) and the mission San Antonio de Valero which became known as the Alamo.
1722	Captain DIEGO RAMÓN founds the mission of Zuníga and its presidio, La Bahía, near the settlement of Goliad.
1746	JOSÉ de ESCANDÓN maps 23 colonies that he founded along the Rio Grande between Tampico and the San Antonio River.
1767	MARQUÉS de RUBÍ crosses Texas from west to east while inspecting the entire northern frontier of New Spain from California to Louisiana.
1778	**ATHANASE de MÉZIÈRES** completes the last major exploration in Texas.

Bibliography

Bolton, Herbert E., *Athanase de Mezieres and the Louisiana-Texas Frontier, 1768-1780*, The Arthur H. Clark Company, Cleveland, 1914.

_____, *Spanish Borderlands*, Volume 23 of *Chronicles of America*, U.S. Publishers.

Carter, Hodding, *Doomed Road of Empire: The Spanish Trail of Conquest*, New York, 1963.

Fehrenbach, T. R., *Lone Star: A History of Texas & Texans*, Macmillan, New York, 1985.

Horgan, Paul, *Great River: The Rio Grande in North American History*, Texas Classics Series, Lone Star Books, 1984.

Nunez Cabeza De Vaca, Alvar, *The Narrative of Alvar Nunez Cabeza Vaca*, Translated by Fanny Bandelier, The Imprint Society, Barre, Mass., 1972.

Parkman, Francis, *Discovery of the Great West: LaSalle*, Edited by William R. Taylor, Greenwood Press, 1986.

Perrigo, Lynn Irwin, *Texas and Our Spanish Southwest*, Banks Upshaw, Dallas, 1960.

Editors of Time-Life, *Spanish West,* from *Old West Series*, Time-Life Books, New York, 1976.

Vivian, Julia, *Cavalier in Texas*, San Antonio, 1953.

Weddle, Robert S., *Wilderness Manhunt: The Spanish Search for LaSalle*, University of Texas Press, Austin, 1973.

Index